LIFE AFTER BIRTH
Spirituality for College Students

WILLIAM TOOHEY

THE SEABURY PRESS · NEW YORK

1981
The Seabury Press
815 Second Avenue
New York, N.Y. 10017

Printed in the United States of America

Library of Congress Cataloging in Publication Data
Toohey, William.   Life after birth.
1. College students—Religious life. I. Title.
BX2373.S8T59   248.4′8203   80–17268
ISBN 0–8164–2290–7

Second printing

To Jane, Joe, Fitz, Sally, Austin, Dan and Tom, colleagues in campus ministry, and the many students who, while allowing me to touch their lives, reciprocated (often unknowingly) and offered me a large measure of life after birth.

Contents

A Personal Preliminary

Shortly after I was asked to write this book, I sought the advice of several students whose judgment I respect.

"Avoid long chapters," they told me. "Write short pieces, brief essays. That way we can make use of the frequent brief intervals we get for this kind of reading, and even if a particular essay doesn't hit on an issue of special concern to us at the moment—no big deal—we can easily pass on to the next one."

They requested commentaries on the questions that are most critical for them. Like the following: Is true happiness attainable? Does God really care? What is faith? Where does Jesus fit in? Am I in college to learn skills or how to be a better person? Is the risk of loving worthwhile? Does success mean making money? What is prayer? Is there anything to hope for? How do we handle friendship and sex? How can God permit evil and suffering? Why confess your sins to a priest? What does love of neighbor have to do with the transformation of structures? Why be a Catholic?

I remember being told of a student's coming up to a priest I know, after his homily, and saying: "I appreciated your little talk, Father. It's good to know your opinion. But does Jesus have anything to say to me today? That's the question. Does He have a word to speak to me, to help make some sense out of my life, to assist me in seeing and understanding what really counts?" I'll always re-member that, and the recollection has influenced this book and its effort to examine some of the many important questions students ask today.

The final words are mine, of course. But they come only after a lot of study and reflection on the words of a great many others, including not a few students. All of this in an attempt to provide, despite the risk involved, a channel for what God has to say to young adults today: "I have come that you might have life . . . and have it to the full!"

1

The Impossible Question

The pattern keeps repeating. Over and over again. As soon as people find out that you live and work with college students, they want to know, "What are college students like these days?"

I used to think I was supposed to give some simplistic overview, a neat encapsulation of the "average" student. Well, maybe I was. But I soon found out how stupid it is to think such a thing is possible.

I've become thoroughly convinced that it is crazy to get caught in the trap of generalizing. I find myself awfully uncomfortable with people who casually make incredible claims—the researcher, for example, who professes to hold the key to the secrets about "the youth of today"; or the administrator who talks to ten students a month, and thinks he knows "the student mind."

In her controversial book, *Liberal Parents, Radical Children,* Midge Decter writes about the collegians of the '60s, celebrated by Charles Reich and Paul Goodman, liberated by Timothy Leary, saluted in song by the Beatles. She examines their fears, their weaknesses, and their inordinate dependencies; and she shows why these children, now that they are in their late twenties and early thirties, "are not in good shape."

Dr. Herbert Hendin, a psychoanalyst from Columbia University, recently completed a six-year study of the

1

current generation of college students. He says they are characterized by the pursuit of disengagement, detachment, fragmentation, and emotional numbness. This means, Hendin maintains, that today's students are "in revolt against love." They believe personal involvement invites disaster, that life is a trap, and attachments make the trap tighter.

Sociologist Andrew Greeley seems to agree, going so far as to suggest that "the best and brightest of our much praised younger generation tend to be something pretty much like sociopaths in their relationships with one another." Greeley refers to certain caricatures of honest sexuality and the struggle for women's rights, and cites them as responsible for untold harm. He speaks about the ideology of "permissiveness" requiring young men to act like chauvinists, and also the ideology of "liberated women," demanding that young females act like castrating witches.

Dr. L. Lamont's *Campus Shock* compiles the horrors revealed in interviews conducted in the eight Ivy League schools, plus the University of Chicago, Michigan, Stanford, and Berkeley. They make it clear that cheating is a way of life. By 1976 only half the undergraduates at Stanford, for example, would say they thought cheating was unjustifiable. In one year 4,500 books were stolen from the Berkeley library. Once caught, college thieves and cheaters tended to say, "I didn't do anything that everyone else isn't doing." Nor were the faculties much better. Many objected to taking a moral stand for fear of "sounding like scolds" to their students. As a University of Chicago professor admitted, "We lack the language to teach right and wrong."

Well, that's a sample of some of the things the "experts" are saying these days about youth. It is

2

probably important to keep up on this sort of analysis, yet I can't help wondering how much understanding the sweeping generalizations contain. I feel about them somewhat the way I do about some religious surveys—"How many students go to Mass in your chapel each Sunday?" Suppose you found out. How much does this "evidence" really tell you—about a person's faith or spiritual life?

So when someone asks, "What is the typical college student like?" I am inclined to say there is no such thing. "Come out to the school," I want to tell them, "and spend a year or more, and even then you won't fully know."

A friend told me recently that he has been asked to write a book "on youth." We agreed about the impracticality of such a project. How do you write a book about youth? Maybe individual youths; maybe about Jim, Mary, Bob, Judy, and Mike and real students you've known, with every possible temperament, personality, value system and human characteristic.

However, I do make at least three basic classifications of the contemporary college students I have known.

One group I would characterize as the "indifferent-alienated." These are the students who are sour and hostile, suspicious and cynical and unresponsive. Lacking profoundly transforming experiences, they float through four years of college without any significant spiritual growth or personality maturation. Frequently they arrive at school thoroughly spoiled, pampered, boorish, inconsiderate, intolerant of any difficulty in life, committed principally to materialistic goals that are self-centered and even downright hedonistic. They strive to avoid vulnerability at all costs, particularly through avoiding self-disclosing, personal relationships.

The next category I would classify the "disengaged-unenlightened." Students in this group have not yet experienced real Christian commitment. Uninformed and unformed they are, but not unreceptive to the proper approach. There is great potential here: a basic goodness and spiritual questing. In some externals, students in this category might be said to resemble their older brothers and sisters of the late sixties and early seventies. But one does not sense in them the anger of those years. On the contrary, theirs is a readiness to explore important questions like faith and God, sin and social involvement. As a theology professor put it, "I find a good number of students amazingly receptive these days. They are not interested in pious platitudes but are very much interested in how the Christian tradition can help them understand themselves."

A final group is the "committed." They have reached some degree of positive conscious Christian commitment. They range from those who manifest decisions for discipleship, however tenuous, to those who are, for their age, truly mature in faith, who have given themselves, with clarity and purpose, both to the person and to the mission of Jesus. You will see them enthusiastically participating in Sunday Eucharist. You also will see them fully involved in volunteer services, helping the poor, the elderly, the retarded, visiting nursing homes, tutoring ghetto children, etc.

Thus I have to admit that there are some who do seem to fit the category of either chauvinists or castrating witches. But there are also the many who dare to love and care for others, involving themselves in the terrifying and exciting risks of human intimacy.

You hear a senior woman student say, "If one more dumb underclassman comes up and tries to introduce himself, I'm going to throw up!" And, in almost the next instant, you overhear another tell how rewarding it was to work on Freshman Orientation. One students tears an article out of a reserve book, thereby shafting all the others who were planning to do the same assignment; while another gives away his football ticket so an inner-city youngster can see the game.

So it goes. We look at them and see some of the most generous/selfish, childish/mature, self-centered/outgoing, hopeful/cynical, considerate/boorish, abusive/gentle people in the whole world.

Maybe that's the point. There is a whole world here—a world of variety. And perhaps we need to remind ourselves how important it is to respect that. We are each unique and this is indistinguishable from our dignity as special creations of God.

I feel more at home with this concept. It seems more real than fanciful exercises in answering impossible questions. It's much better to respect uniqueness and celebrate individuality . . . and believe that it can lead somehow to finding true communion in the one who is Father to us all.

2

Is There Life after Birth?

I received an unusual note from a student one Easter. The stationery unfolded into a long single sheet, and running along the left-hand margin were footprints. The young woman explained that these, for her, were the footprints of Jesus walking away from the tomb on Easter.

In the course of the letter, she extended to me an Easter wish—one of the nicest I've ever received. She said: "I hope you discover empty tombs all the days of your life."

She explained what she meant by this. If I were to be the kind of person she thought I wanted to be, it would mean that I had really entered other people's lives in such a way that they were touched and lifted, rescued and freed from whatever was holding them back from authentic life. Consequently, I should be able to observe empty tombs as a kind of testimonial to the fact that people had been raised and brought to a greater life through the force of the relationship we had had.

I have thought a lot about what she said, and now I'm beginning to wonder if we haven't had our thinking changed around. We presume that we spend a lifetime walking toward the tomb, but I'm speculating now that it's just the opposite. We spend our whole lives walking away from the tomb.

What I'm trying to say is this? When we are born, we are not, by that very fact, automatically alive. Being born is simply to begin the process either of coming alive or going towards entombment. From the very first moments of our existence, we are affected constantly by one or other of two forces, either the creative force of love or the crushing force of unlove (what Albert Camus called the plague). From that first instance, we are either affirmed or denied in our relationships with one another. Consequently, the tomb is a very definite threat in *this* life. We need either to be rescued from it or, if we've been lucky enough so far to escape it, to remain free from its trap.

There is a real paradox involved here. The movement towards life, once you are born, can only happen through experiencing death. Even birth itself, for example, is a kind of death. The child has to be willing to die to a life he or she has known for nine months, with all its security, comfort, total dependence. And from that moment on, there begins a never-ending series of deaths-in-order-to-know-life experiences.

Take the day we went off to school for the first time—leaving the second womb, the home. We entered a larger experience of life, met other children, had new adventures, further ruptures of former times of safety and freedom from risk and vulnerability. There were a lot of moments of dying in those days (I remember them well!), but they always led to greater life. So, too, does coming to college, which is another death to former securities and attitudes and life-style.

Somewhere along the way, if we are lucky, we learn the profound truth contained in a simple saying: "The pledge of your heart is the beginning of your death." The moment you pledge your heart to anything, and especially to any*one,* you necessarily begin to die—to whatever stands between you and fidelity to that pledge.

Whenever we say "yes" to a project, a new value, a

principle, a career decision, or to another person in friendship, we know it is going to cost us something. And this will be like a dying. But the death is really a putting to death of apathy, indifference, comfort, convenience, all those things which are obstacles to the pledge we've made.

The temptation will be to avoid those deaths. Psychologically, it is like sucking your thumb, that is, trying to have circumstances be as they were earlier in life, more invulnerable to the present costly demands of growth through deaths to fuller life. But the paradox works both ways: advancement towards life can only happen through deaths; progression into death inevitably follows from efforts to escape death.

This basic growth pattern doesn't suddenly and magically cease when you graduate from college, although many students I've known have labored under that delusion.

The earlier experiences don't depart. They just broaden with adulthood. One day, for example, one knows a new kind of dying-in-order-to-live; not as an infant, adolescent or young adult, but as the *parent* of one.

3

Feeling No Pain

College students who get smashed, bombed, blind-drunk on a weekend may reveal more than they realize in the admission, "I was feeling no pain!"

Actually, what is frequently revealed is an experience of the pain of death we've just been speaking about. Thus pain is an unavoidable consequence of the human condition. And we've got to come to grips with it. C.S. Lewis was right: "Pain insists upon being attended to." We are forced to deal with it, live with it, try to ride it through. It's necessary to the maturing process. When we can't understand this, we get caught up in all kinds of escape efforts, trying to kill the pain. But efforts to avoid the inevitable pain of facing life head-on are doomed to failure.

Suicide, which has an alarmingly high rate among young adults, is the ultimate (and literal) effort to kill the pain. It happened not so long ago to a former student of mine. His mother sent me a copy of the letter he left with his family. In her note to me she said: "Perhaps by studying his letter you may be able to keep some other young person from doing what my son did."

I'm not at all sure I can. For one thing, the letter is not all that coherent. I still shudder every time I read it. It begins: "Dear Family. I'm sorry to disturb your dinner; I'm sure what I have to say will not elicit toasts of 'cheerio.' You see, I have terminated my life."

Throughout the letter there are incessant revelations of pain: frustrations over peer associations, distress at the presence of great oppression and evil in the world, and the deep hurt suffered as a result of a rejection by the girl he loved. Everywhere there is a sense of self-loathing—a basic inability to befriend himself and successfully to handle the pain resulting from honest self-confrontation.

Why do people hate themselves this way, feel uncomfortable with the persons they are, find it difficult to like what they see in themselves? It seems that what we experience in our relationships with others contributes greatly to our self-concept. Rollo May is probably right: self-knowledge doesn't come from our self-scrutiny, but is a gift from others. Our treatment of one another communicates a sense of personal value. We notice, for example, how often a friend will measure up to the expectations that others hold for him.

Public television once did a documentary on black children in a grade-school art class. They were asked to draw pictures of themselves. Again and again the self-portraits were faceless. Their self-concept was negative because no one had ever given them signs that they were of value. It's true: people will conform to our expectations. I remember a student I was once counseling. "My mother," the young woman said, "has always failed to trust me. She is constantly telling me that I'm no good and that I will not amount to anything. I've had it with her. I'm tempted now to give her the kind of performance from me that she always expected." When she said that, she was a good, innocent person. But soon afterward she began secretly to date a married man (mostly to spite her mother), and has since gone steadily down hill.

We correctly understand that we will not feel good about ourselves unless others concur in their opinions of us and show it in the way they deal with us. Unfortunately, there is a danger of adopting the false notion that our self-worth is established when we can point to external credentials—accomplishments, achievements, acquisitions.

We may believe these externals provide documentation of our self-worth, and impel anyone who judges fairly to acknowledge the fact. We hear ourselves arguing something like this: I will never feel significant unless I do something significant. Therefore my strategy is as follows: *Do* something important, *be* someone important, *feel* important.

This is the contemporary heresy of salvation through achievement and accomplishment. It has infected our whole culture. Typically, we feel it is only by achieving that a person becomes something, that he amounts to something significant. Isn't this our experience? Don't we recognize our society measuring success and self-worth by achievements?

The worst thing that can be said of anyone, according to the conventional wisdom of the day, is that he has achieved nothing. Work, career, earning money—what could be more important? Industrializing, producing, expanding, growth, progress, perfection—is this not the meaning of life?

How is a man or a woman to justify his or her existence if not by achievements? Modern life sets a premium on achieving, continuing to progress, being more and more successful. Since a human being must constantly justify his existence, he must achieve. I spent a long time with a student who wanted to go to Mexico on an apostolic project because he felt that then he would feel good about himself. It took a lot of conversation and reflection before he began to consider the possibility that the proper attitude was just the opposite. First he ought to feel good about himself and then, *because of that*, consider the possibility of traveling to Mexico to give himself in service to others.

Suppose you meet someone you haven't seen for a while. She asks, "How are you?" Don't you soon find yourself answering her question as though she had asked, "What have you done? What tangible signs can you point to in proof of your worth today?" Consequently, people identify themselves to one another in terms of status, job position, salary, material acquisitions, what clubs they belong to, where they vacation, etc. It's what they've done, what they've got—that is who they are! As Californians put it, "You *are* what you drive!"

The former chaplain at Yale, William Sloane Coffin, illustrates how ridiculous the whole thing can become: "I knew a guy who was very happy living in Pelham, N.Y., but he got promoted so he thought he had to move to Pelham Manor. Then they promoted him again, and so he had to cross the Connecticut border into Darien or Greenwich. Now he has to commute much farther than he used to, he sees his kids much less, but he's living where it counts. These days the neighborhood tells us who we are. It's pathetic."

I've been associated with many college graduates who painfully discovered the emptiness of this sort of life vision. When they define success in materialistic terms, they opt for the morally vacuous, the spiritually bankrupt. Consequently, there is the distinct possibility that one may be *doing* very well (according to one's bankbook) without *being* very well. There is a kind of private hell in this choice of how you live your life. It can only lead to dead-end despair, frustration, depression. And all because of a simple, crucial fact: real self-worth cannot be

12

acquired through accomplishments. It simply cannot be achieved.

I made an important discovery in John Shea's fine book, *Stories of God*. Shea makes the point that "the need to validate ourselves in an ultimate way, and the fear that we will not, disappears before the Spirit-created consciousness that our self-worth is a gift of God."

When I first read and reflected on that sentence, especially the final phrase, I figured Father Shea meant it in the sense that self-worth is a gift *from* God; that is, God tells us (in many ways) that we are of extreme worth to Him. We are precious. We are sons and daughters. We are heirs of the kingdom, brothers and sisters to Jesus, made in the image and likeness of God, His supreme achievement of creation.

Still, I was puzzled by the phraseology. If that's what Shea meant, why did he say "of" instead of "from" God? Then I realized that, although it is indeed true that a sense of our self-worth comes *from* God's communicating the fact to us, there is more. The most important reason for our self-worth is that we have the gift *of* God. What Father Shea said is literally true. God has given us, not just information about our self-worth, but Himself!

In answer to the question, "In what is your self-worth?" I don't need to look to anything like achievements or other externals. The answer is much simpler—and magnificent. I have self-worth because I have God. God has given me Himself. He has come to me, dwells within me, as Jesus promised.

It is this realization that is meant to sustain us as we endure the inevitable pain of growth and self-confrontation. Having God's life within us, how can we not feel a sense of worth?

4

When Nothing Is the Same

Notre Dame's brilliant theologian, John Dunne, tells a fascinating story he calls "The Parable of the Mountain." In it he describes a man climbing a mountain at the top of which, he thinks, is God. By climbing the mountain and reaching God, the man anticipates that he will leave the pain of his shallow, empty life behind in the valley, from which he has escaped. But while he climbs, God is coming down the mountain, down into the valley, down amidst the toil and grief. In the mists of the mountain, God and man pass one another.

When the man reaches the mountain top he will find nothing. God is not there. What then will he do? He realizes his climb was a mistake. But what now? Agony and despair? Or will he turn to retrace his path, through the mists, into the valley, to where God has gone seeking him?

"Where God has gone seeking him"—this is the key. This is the very heart of the mystery of life. Religion, for example, is not so much our quest for God, but God's search for us. That is what it means to be a Chosen People. Not that by some piety or accomplishment we have raised ourselves up over other people to a place of eminence, but that, in spite of our frailties and betrayals, God reaches out to choose us.

We object. That's not our experience, being chosen like

14

that. Our experience is just the opposite, many of us. We are much more aware of *not* being chosen. Like the seniors who go through the job-interview routine and *don't* get chosen, or the many students who are not chosen for med school, dental school, law school. The students, for example, during room-pick time who don't get chosen by anyone; or the ones never asked to a formal or dorm party or concert; or those who don't even hear an occasional, "Do you want to go over to lunch?"

All of us know that experience of not being chosen. It's something we endure throughout life. Remember how it was when you were a child? There were so many occasions of choosing. When boys in grade school, for instance, would choose up sides for baseball.

You'd stand in the schoolyard with a mob of about twenty kids, and the two captains would start choosing sides. As names were called out, and yours wasn't one of them, it really got to you. Since selection was on the basis of talent and ability, not being chosen said something about what others thought of you. I can remember standing there, praying that my name would be called. The worst experience of all, of course, was to be left to the end, especially when the sides were even without you. Then it really got humiliating. One captain would say, "I've got all I need. You take him." And the other would respond, "No, that's all right. You can have him."

In the midst of these recollections of how often we are not chosen, God would have us believe that He doesn't operate that way. He chooses each of us by name. We are each chosen first, and there are no conditions whatsoever. We find this hard to swallow. It's difficult to believe God would choose us, since we have so many experiences of not being chosen by anyone else—even ourselves.

Of course, there is that strange man, Jesus, who was

always choosing the "unchoosable." He constantly sought out the hurting, suffering, fearful, ordinary women and men, whose lives, more often than not, appeared futile and directionless.

Take the good thief. I like to think that, in some way, he stands for each of us. He, too, had been running away from the pain of life, thinking that this was the way to find happiness. What a mess he had made of it. And yet his yearning, I suspect, was like that of the poet, Anne Sexton, who, in her collection of poems entitled *The Awful Rowing Toward God*, wrote:

> And God was there like an island
> I had not rowed to,
> still ignorant of him,
> my arms and legs worked,
> and I grew, I grew
> I wore rubies and bought tomatoes
> and now, in my middle age,
> about nineteen in the head I'd say
> I am rowing, I am rowing

All the time the good thief had been searching for happiness, he didn't know that Happiness had been looking for him. That's why the story of this bandit is the story of many of us. The quest for happiness (or the effort to escape from pain) is the quest for God. But He is the one who finds us first. That's why Christianity is good news. We don't pursue happiness, it pursues us.

"He touched me," Barbra Streisand sings; "he really meant to do it; he touched me and nothing is the same." This is most especially true with respect to God. Since the time of Abraham, God has reached out to touch people, involving Himself in human history. In Jesus, God's touch achieves the greatest intimacy, the most tender, personal involvement. We are stunned and startled, and indeed thrilled, as we realize that this is what has happened to us. Our self-worth (for which we crave) is a gift of God. "In the midst of winter, I finally learned that there was in me an invincible summer," Albert Camus once wrote.

Funny how God always exceeds the boundaries of our imaginations. He always refuses to be limited by our understanding. He waits to surprise us with His touch, to overwhelm us with the unfathomed depth of His love. He touches us, and nothing is the same!

5

Where Does Jesus Come In?

We Christians are convinced of Jesus' divinity. But we also believe that He was truly human. That meant, George McCauley suggests, "no capitalizing on His divine connections, no escape clauses, no end-arounds. While we believe this in theory, the way we sometimes read Scripture indicates that, in practice, we think Jesus is just going through the human motions, while a conspiratorial wink of one divine eye."

Consider that scene between Jesus and Peter, when Jesus asks the question, "Who do people say that the Son of Man is?" This is no coy, multiple-choice examination of Peter's catechetical knowledge. There is no reason not to believe Jesus was sincere. If He asked a question, why couldn't it be because He Himself was puzzled about the impression He is giving others?

We can truly identify with that. There is hardly anything a person is more interested in than the opinions and impressions of others (and this is true, it seems, in a particular way for college students). We may be a bit frightened to find out the truth, but still we have a great curiosity about what other people think of us: "What do they say when they talk about me? What do my friends really think of me?"

It's perfectly normal to believe that Jesus shared that human condition, and so Peter's answer provides affirmation and clarification for Jesus, of the sort our best friends can give us.

Peter says in effect: "I see what everyone sees, Your wisdom, Your power, determination, courage, compassion. I put it all together and conclude that You are not simply a prophet but the fulfillment of prophecy. You are the Christ, the presence of God Himself in our midst."

I once saw a billboard, which proclaimed in large letters: "Christ is the answer." Someone had climbed up and painted across the bottom, "What is the question?" Well, we know there is not just one question. The thrilling revelation shared with us is that Jesus is the answer to those several deepest, most significant questions we ask: Is God around? Does He care? Does He involve Himself in my life? Does He lead me through the struggles, challenges and frightening experiences I have? How can I find happiness in life? How can I live forever?

Jesus is the answer to all those questions. One way He provides the answer is as Good Shepherd.

The prophets of the Old Testament were forced to deliver scathing indictments against their leaders—wicked shepherds, they called them: "You have failed to make the weak sheep strong or to care for the sick ones, or bandage the wounded. You have failed to bring back the strays or look for the lost. On the contrary, you have ruled them cruelly and violently" (Ezekiel 34:4).

It was the same in Jesus' day. He called the leaders hirelings who abandoned the flock and betrayed the people. Obviously, we wonder about our own day, as we note the distressing similarity, as we observe countless leaders who still continue to refuse people their rightful role in their own church, who are pompous, self-serving and arrogant.

Regrettably, we are forced to agree with biblical

scholar Father John McKenzie, who writes: "The Roman Catholic church has recently shown once again that its highest levels of government are unacquainted with even fair and honest use of power."

In our distress and pain over the failure of church leadership, we hardly know what to say. Then we discover that we don't have to say anything. God does. He says more than enough: "I have seen the miserable state of My people; I have heard their appeal to be free of their slave-drivers. Yes, I am well aware of their sufferings. I mean to deliver them" (Exodus 3:7-8).

God has planned that He Himself would speak a word of response to our situation, and that Word is Jesus. Jesus came to correct the failures of leadership of those false shepherds. Jesus is the Good Shepherd, fulfilling in His actions the promise of the Father: "I Myself will pasture My sheep. I will give them rest; I will search out and find the lost; I will heal the wounded. I will shepherd them rightly" (Ezekiel 34:15-16).

Jesus' mission is to enflesh and make tangible this shepherding God whom, heretofore, no one had ever experienced quite this way. Remember how St. John put it? "No one has ever seen God, not at any time. His only begotten Son has Himself become our interpreter" (John 1:18). The Father's plan was that Jesus would replace the false leaders of the people, and would Himself continue to personally minister, even after His resurrection and ascension, through His disciples. The present failures of our church simply document the fact that many of us resist the risen Jesus who wishes to reach out to humans through us, as He did 2,000 years ago.

Jesus revealed Himself as a man who loved, who was tender and sensitive to the needs of others, who showed kindness and generosity and was unafraid to shed tears over the death of a friend; a man who unapologetically revealed His emotions and His deep affection for women and men, young and old.

I recall being in a student discussion group when, after we had been examining the way Jesus related to people, a young woman in the group suddenly said: "You know, God is very Christlike." We all smiled when she said that, but then realized how accurate a statement it was. How do we really know what God is like? Too often men dreamed up their fancy concepts (unmoved mover, *ens subsistens,* omnipotent creator) and laid them on God. We had it all backwards. First, one needs to discover Jesus, who is the revealer of God. Then one can say, "Oh, that is what God is like. How wonderful. Just the kind of God I would want to have, should anyone ever ask me. I could give myself to someone like that. Christlike!"

21

6

Even upon the Stones

"God did not make death, nor does He rejoice in the destruction of the living. For He fashioned all things that they might have being" (Wisdom 1:13-14).

Try giving that little speech, standing before the parents, roommates and friends of students taken from us in untimely death. That's just got to be the hardest thing for all of us to deal with—I know it is for me.

Our world seems to be going crazy. Signs of death and destruction are everywhere. And often God is blamed. It seems this powerful controversy has been going on forever. In the days of the Old Testament, for example, it might be an individual battle, like the one between God and Job. Later it dealt with Yahweh's relationship with the whole Israelite people, who wrestled with the fact that they, the "chosen people," were regularly overrun by dark forces of irreligion and tyranny.

Thus it's hardly surprising that, until Jesus there was not much progress in eliminating the tendency to blame God for the misery people suffer. God kept saying neat things, but the experience provided contrary evidence. At best, there was a standoff. And then Jesus came.

People watched and experienced what Jesus actually did. He heals this person, then that one. In many ways, He enters into their death-filled lives. In response to human needs, He simply does the most human thing. And that is characteristic of Jesus. Time and again He responds to human needs in a given situation, even if that means running contrary to what others discern as Law or Principle or Morality. Jesus was not, in that sense, a moralist. He simply offered help when people hurt—spontaneously, with compassion, without calculation. But then Jesus Himself is killed; and everything is up for grabs again.

A 7th grader, invited to submit a question to a visiting priest, wrote: "Why would God let His own son suffer on the cross? Was He too chicken to do it Himself? It's like He was sending someone else to do His dirty work."

That says it pretty well. We all wonder about the mystery of God's letting Jesus be crucified. Unfortunately, there has been no end of nonsense offered to explain the mystery. You have one school of thought, for example, that speaks about Jesus "snatching us from the hands of an angry God, buying us back with His blood."

You get the distinct impression that, since people have sinned against God, someone has to be "wasted," so Jesus takes the rap, and somehow the balance of justice is restored. Some have paid an awful price just to make Jesus seem attractive. The Father ends up a wrathful character who needs to be appeased and pacified. He seems to have predetermined a certain amount of pain His son must suffer in order to make satisfaction for all the sins of men and women, as though God were a hard-nosed pawnbroker, holding a ticket on us that can be redeemed only with blood.

What a poisonous image of God, a Father somehow pleased by the fact that Jesus' death was such a bloody painful one. A sadistic God tickled by the suffering of an innocent man, childishly concerned about His own honor, anxious to see it avenged like some Mafia godfather. Such theories, with no support from a proper understanding of Scripture, suggest a monster-god.

On the contrary, nothing that attributes unworthy motives to God can have any part in an explanation of the crucifixion. Any legitimate theology of our salvation and Jesus' crucifixion must begin and end with the fact that God is love. As Gerard Sloyan has pointed out, God is justice also, but His justice is administered lovingly.

Let's say it very clearly. The Father did not want His own son to suffer; He didn't desire or demand bloody satisfaction. All He asked was for Jesus to be true to Him in an obedient and trusting surrender no matter what came His way. The Father had committed Himself to His plan that people should be free, and so this entailed the risk that free persons would misuse their freedom and freely choose to assassinate His beloved son.

To do what the Father asked of Him meant Jesus had to deny Himself what was most natural to want—survival. By freely choosing to refuse escape from the collision course He saw Himself on with the authorities, Jesus achieved exaltation. What the cross reveals is the glorification of a man who obediently accepted death.

Now we are at the final, most important question: What does all of this have to do with our own salvation? How does what Jesus did then save us now?

Well, for one thing, He saves us from missing the whole meaning of life. He would call us to live the way He did, for it is the only way one is saved—by surrendering to the Father and remaining true to that pledge of love no matter what it takes . . . takes from us, takes out of us.

Jesus did what He did, not so that the Father would relent and relinquish His grudge, but so that *we* would relent. He did it so that we would turn away from our violence (revealed in a God of love hung on a tree), and

24

so that we would abandon our resistance to the Father who calls us to Himself. This is how Jesus saves us "through His death on the cross." He saves us from missing the whole meaning of life and from blindness to the loving appeals of a God so amazing that He loves us even when we kill His son.

There is a final way in which Jesus saves us. The cross freed Him for resurrection. It led to His complete availability, His being able to be with us and for us without limitation or restriction. Jesus died and, in resurrection, was free to become the risen Lord for us at this present moment. Jesus reveals the Father's saving power to us now. It is His risen life we share—life beyond disease, infirmity, ashes or grave. The accident or illness or terror that destroys is less powerful than the love within. Jesus would have us know that God desires our living and our salvation even more than we do. He is a God of life. For Him, and for Him alone, death is only a sleep, and His power awakens.

Our yearning to live is but a feeble breath compared to the yearning of God to draw us to Himself, that is, to life. This is the utterly lovely meaning of these lines by D. H. Lawrence. Speaking to everyone who has ever lived, he wrote:

> Thou shalt fight as a flower fighteth
> Upwards through the stones . . .
> To flower in the sun at last.
> For the yearning of the Lord
> Streameth as a sun
> Even upon the stones.

The stones in our lives, all that diminishes life and threatens it, are often sins and anxieties, disappointments, suffering, all the ways we get "dumped on," whatever weighs heavily upon us, and finally the sense of mortality itself. Then the stone becomes a gravestone fitted in place. With Jesus, it sealed His tomb.

But "the yearning of the Lord streameth as a sun *even upon the stones.*" We are delivered from sin, anxiety, suffering, fear, the tomb. Of us the Book of Wisdom speaks: "God formed them to be imperishable; in the image of His own nature He made them."

We are the living, and our God is alive! Then He says it one more time: "Rise up!" And we discover that now we are the ones He is taking by the hand!

7

The God Who Gets Too Close

Right from the start the difference was apparent. When Jesus made His appearance, the major emphasis was not on grim warnings about perdition waiting just around the corner. Instead, His words urgently reveal His great desire to be with people.

In that tremendous scene with Zacheus, we note the astonishing thing He says. Not, "I might condescend to visit you" or "I'm slumming this week and it's your turn today." No, He says, "I *must* come to your house and dine with you." There is a sense of longing. He considers it a favor if this man will offer Him hospitality.

Jesus reveals that our God is not confined in churches, to sacraments, to the words of preachers or the high places of heaven. He is the lover of persons, eager to dwell in the dwelling places of His people: their hearts.

A God like this seems to threaten a lot of people. They would feel much more comfortable with a God who stays in the sky, who is mostly transcendent, remote, and distant. Yet this God is love, and love is the motivation behind all that He has done, from creation to the sending of His son. We can rejoice in realizing the import of the various images of God's love we find in the Bible.

His love is like a father's ("When Israel was a child, then I loved him and called my son out of Egypt"); it is a mother's ("Can a woman forget her nursing child, so as

27

not to have pity on the son of her own womb? Even should this be possible, yet I will never forget you").

Quite understandably, we exult in the fact that God is a seeker of women and men, the "Hound of Heaven." He is always making the first move, always pursuing, always trying to draw closer.

The problem comes when we begin to grasp what kind of a response He desires from us. In reaction to His presence of love, we may revere Him, respect Him, admire Him. But none of that gets at the heart of the matter. He is asking for something quite different. The question (as Peter found out) is: "Do you love me?" God wants a return of love from us. Why should anyone be surprised? This is the expectation we hold when we offer love to one another. Why should God be limited to something less?

This is really what the word "religion" means. It comes from roots that means "to bind together," "to establish a bond or covenant." To say it another way, religion is a relationship, a relationship of love.

This may appear threatening enough (or exciting enough, depending upon your point of view), but there is more. The nature of the relationship of love is not just that of child to parent. Both the Old and New Testaments put it in terms of marriage. Hosea, for example, parallels the relationship between God and us with that of a man and woman coming together after an estrangement and rekindling their love. In this context, God is not father, He is husband. Hosea speaks of a lover seeking his beloved, and making plans for a wedding: "I will espouse you in love and mercy; I will espouse you in fidelity."

Jesus, of course, does not make matters any simpler by using the same image of marriage. Jesus, the manifestation of a God who would establish with us the most intimate of ties, comes into our lives and proposes, in the deepest sense of that word. He proposes a love that is marked by a desire that seeks union with the beloved. He refers to Himself as Bridegroom, seeking intimate union with His bride, the church.

We can immediately see what a problem this causes. In our culture, our unfortunate Anglo-Saxon fundamentalist heritage makes it difficult for us to accept adult-to-adult love in our spirituality. On the contrary, most of us are comfortable only when we can deal with Christian love as either parental or childlike.

So, for some God is a child; they have a special devotion to the Baby Jesus or the Infant of Prague. It is easy to belittle this parent-to-child relationship but what about the reverse emphasis—a child-to-parent focus? If God is *only* Father, then we can never be spiritually mature adults.

The Christian mystics and saints recognized the truth of this. Christian love is not only brotherly or sisterly, fatherly or motherly, it is also the love of the spouse. We may not want this kind of God. It's easier to deal with another kind of God, one who keeps us in line, is strict, an impersonal banker.

In other words, we may refuse His invitation to spiritual adventure. We may pass up His promise: "And you shall know the Lord." We are invited to be in His company, like the disciples with the Bridegroom—free to love the God of our deepest desire and to know that the union does not end with death. No "until death do us part" in this relationship. Quite the contrary. Death becomes that moment when the promise is kept in all its fullness: "I will espouse you to Myself forever."

The famous Greek novelist Nikos Kazantzakis, tells a true story of the occasion when he visited a saintly monk on a remote island. The author asked the monk, "Do you still wrestle with the devil, Fr. Makarios?" "Not any longer, my child. I have grown old and the devil has grown old with me. He doesn't have the strength. I now wrestle with God." "With God," Kazantzakis exclaimed, astonished. "And you hope to win?" "No," the monk answered. "I hope to lose!"

When I first read that story, I thought how revealing it was of my own situation: I have been fighting God for a long time—fighting Him off! Maybe that's the problem. Perhaps it's time to lose!

8

Breath or Suffocation

The Campus Ministry office, where I work, is affection-
ately referred to as The Zoo, meaning it harbors all kinds
of strange and beautiful animals. There is seldom a dull
moment, so we are not easily interrupted or silenced by
anything. But the other day something happened that
momentarily startled the entire crowd.

One of my colleagues was called to the telephone; and
the next thing we knew she was exclaiming: "Right now?
Over the phone!" You can imagine how that stilled the
room. After the call was completed she told us: "This
woman I've never met before gets me on the phone and
immediately blurts out, 'Will you please tell me—what is
the Holy Spirit?' "

That's not a bad question, even though it may be a bit
disconcerting to get it in the middle of a hectic day of
dealing with more mundane problems. We Catholics
believe we know the answer. We know at least a dozen
answers, as a matter of fact, and they are all correct. The
Holy Spirit is the Third Person of the Trinity, the gift of
the Father and Son, the Paraclete, the Advocate, the
Indwelling Spirit, and the Presence of the Living God.

I recently ran across an additional description. A
Catholic theologian and educator put it this way: "The
Holy Spirit is the surprise in life. The Spirit surprises us all
the time." I was reminded of the line from the playwright,

31

Ugo Betti: "To believe in God is to know that all the rules will be fair, and that there will be wonderful surprises."

How true! God's Spirit does have surprises in store for us. The first surprise is something we may have sensed but did not realize the Scriptures supported so strongly: The Spirit of God will not "play according to our rules," will not conform to or be controlled by our systems.

Remember what Jesus did when He greeted His apostles after His resurrection? He breathed on them. And how they needed it! He gave them breath (Spirit) at the very moment they were suffocating to death. The Pentecost Spirit (breath) of God is a generating principle of life that transforms persons who are isolated, cold, wooden, and dead into a people filled with color and life.

Suffocation abounded at that time, and still does. People in our towns and cities and chanceries are wound up so tight one wonders if there is even room for the Spirit. How can a fresh breath, like the Spirit, get in? How can there be a place for the noisy, strong, driving wind that is God's Spirit? If the Spirit wants to breathe, they imply, let it happen through proper channels. For those who suffocate, there is little room for festival, poetry, dreaming, innovation, creativity, or prophetic witness.

One of their favorite words is "inopportune." It's used all the time by ecclesiastical bureaucrats. According to a directive from Rome, for example, it was decreed "inopportune" for the American bishops to endorse a recent proposal that U.S. corporations discontinue investments in racist South Africa.

The workings of the Holy Spirit, then, are supremely inopportune. The Spirit is very hard to domesticate and control, as those churchmen are discovering who, so unsure of themselves as persons, take refuge in office and behind ecclesiastical rank against those (especially women) who are so "misguided" that they are trying to force their way into full membership in their own church.

The Holy Spirit also surprises us by refusing to be limited to our boundaries. I refer to the fact that, although the Spirit does act within the institution of the Roman Catholic church, there is no limitation to "authorized ecclesiastical channels." The Spirit is not given only through official channels. God does not use only identifiable believers to be recipients of His gift of the Spirit.

You may recall the Gospel incident when the apostle John was distressed because a man who was not a disciple of Jesus was using Jesus' name to heal people. John wanted Jesus to stop the man. But Jesus rejected such a limited understanding of the Spirit's activity. God is not limited to His church or to His believers or Scriptures, when He desires to reveal Himself or accomplish His purpose in the world, as if, as a friend of mine once put it, "the Lord Himself can't call an audible at the line of scrimmage if He wants to."

There is only one way God is limited: He must act for the sake of His kingdom, which means all creation. The kingdom of God is a lot broader and more encompassing than many of us may think. God's intervention and saving presence through His Spirit is for all, not just the Catholic church and, indeed, not just all the Christian churches.

We must forever put to rest that heresy that claims there is no salvation outside the church. The church and the kingdom of God are not synonymous. There *is* salvation outside the church precisely because God is outside. His Spirit cannot be confined. The Catholic church, for example, cannot lay claim to every branch on that mustard tree Jesus used as an illustration of His kingdom; it is only one of the branches.

The whole world may not, in fact, become the church,

but it must become incorporated into the kingdom. It must, that is, experience the presence of the reign of God and His creative love, without which no person will be able to know the full life to which we are called.

The universality of the kingdom and the unlimited range of God's Spirit are offensive to many, who resent the fact that the Father's love goes out indiscriminately to everyone. You may have read Flannery O'Connor's fascinating short story, "Revelation." As it opens, a certain Mrs. Turpin sits in a doctor's waiting room judging the acceptable and unacceptable people around her. Later in the day, she returns to her farm and is going about her chores. In the glow of the setting sun, she has a vision of a bridge swinging from earth to heaven. On the bridge a large crowd of souls is mounting to heaven. This company is made up of all those types Mrs. Turpin passed judgment on in the courtroom of her mind: "White trash, clean for the first time in their lives, and bands of blacks in white robes, and battalions of freaks and lunatics shouting and clapping and leaping like frogs."

The rear of the procession is made up of people like Mrs. Turpin and her husband, who have always used the wits God gave them. This group strides the bridge "with great dignity, accountable as they had always been for good order and common sense and respectable behavior. They alone were on key."

What surprises are in store for us! Our present attitude determines whether, on that final day, we will be surprised with delight because we see so many who were considered in their lifetime "outside the company"— unworthy of the kingdom—or whether we will be surprised with the horror of not being there ourselves.

God continues to prove that He does not share Mrs. Turpin's discriminating taste. He is still the friend of the unwanted, the dead-enders, the outcasts, the losers, the nobodies, the forgotten and despised—those whom any respectable person would shun. We perhaps hear ourselves mouthing familiar words: "How is it You associate with sinners, and even dine with them?"

If our god is too small, it is because *we* are. That kind of god is not the true God who said: "I will draw all persons to Myself; I will pour out My Spirit upon all flesh. Whoever calls upon the name of the Lord shall be saved."

That's the temptation: to make our kingdom narrow, exclusive, limited, and cramped. But that only makes us eligible for a repeat of what Jesus had to say the first time: "You people shut the kingdom of heaven against others." On the contrary, we should rejoice that His kingdom is as large as it is—even big enough for us!

9

Something Even Nonbelievers Can Believe In

A young woman came to see me. Without any hesitation, she came right out with what was on her mind: "I don't believe in God. Convince me."

What do you say when someone does that? Well, if you're smart, you don't say anything. You let the other person say; that is, you let them speak and tell their story. And what a story it was.

She was born in the inner city of Chicago. She never knew her father. Whoever he was, he was never married to her mother. She lived with her mother, but never knew a mother's love. Nor did it take long to discover the truth about the long series of "uncles" who periodically stayed with them.

Growing up in this kind of jungle, surrounded by bitterness and contempt, the young woman explained how she built up a hard shell of self-defense. In the beginning she had opened herself to others, as a naive, unsuspecting child will do. She had hoped and trusted, but soon found out the hard way that she was just asking for heartbreak. People, she discovered, are out to get what they can, interested only in themselves, and if you let them they will use you.

She told how, as she advanced into her teens, she

became an object of interest for men. But that was just the problem. She was merely an object, a source of recreation ("It's cheaper than bowling if you can get someone who's willing"). She soon got a reputation as a "Kleenex girl"—you use them, then throw them away. Eventually, she said, she felt the only way to survive was to withdraw into herself.

Then one day in the summer she met, quite by chance, a young graduate student who was working in the ghetto as part of his field experience in social studies. His background had been much different from hers. He had grown up in surroundings of love and understanding and trust and, consequently, he was a loving, warm person. When he saw her, he greeted her with a friendly smile. But she gave him one of those if-looks-could-kill glances in return. This didn't put him off, however, and he continued to say hello when he saw her day after day. For a time, she just glowered at him, but little by little his warmth and openness began to penetrate her shell.

She chanced a nod, then a day or so later, a mumbled "Hi." She thought he probably was going to turn out just like all the other men she had known, even though, being a grad student his tactics might be more subtle, his approach more low-key.

But he was simply a good man whose heart had gone out to her quite spontaneously, with understanding and compassion. She couldn't believe he was honestly interested in her, just for herself, but she began to hope against hope that what seemed to be might actually prove to be true.

At this point in her narrative, she described a strange and marvelous transformation that began to take place. To the degree she allowed the power of the young man's friendship into her life, she began to blossom as a person.

Her rough, vulgar language got cleaned up, she became more concerned about personal appearance, and, more importantly, a new inner light began to show.

The young man, as it turned out, wasn't just playing social worker. He was truly interested, he cared, he gave himself. Through her responses to his gift of friendship, she was led to ever more involving commitments and acts of confidence and trust. It became very painful, for she eventually found herself forced to turn away from all her old convictions and attitudes—the way she thought she had to be for survival's sake.

At the end of that summer, the young man declared his feelings: "I care for you very much." In so doing, however, he forced the issue. She was brought to the brink. If she acknowledged that she felt the same way about him, she would be opening herself again, after swearing she would never again become so vulnerable. There had already been too many rejections in the past. This one would really kill her.

After a torturous struggle that was like dying to all she had built up to protect herself, she took the plunge. She surrendered her heart in an honest admission of her feelings for him. It was like jumping off a cliff, yet somehow she felt richer for it. And he wasn't kidding. It was for real, what he had said, all that he had become for her during these months. She had come back from the dead, freed from the tomb of unlove where she had been imprisoned.

I was so moved by her story that I found it hard to concentrate on the original question. "Although you say you don't believe in God," I began, "it does seem obvious that you believe in love." "Oh yes," she said, "I've seen its power in my own life, and I would like to live that way, too, giving myself in friendship to others who might need me." "Your story," I continued, "reminds me of the line in the song, "Alfie": 'I believe in love, Alfie; something even nonbelievers can believe in.' I would like to think I could say the same thing, that I believe in love. When I say that, however, I'm convinced that it also means that I believe in God, for God *is* love. Maybe you can't see that, maybe you can't accept that connection right now, and, if so, that's okay—everyone's timing is different. If you've allowed love into your life, especially through the friendship of that young man, and if God is love, then who is to say that God's life is not within you? You may not think you believe in God and, indeed, you may not explicitly acknowledge His existence or be able to offer detailed information about Him or know anything about Jesus and His church. But you have taken the crucial first step, without which no one ever comes to full life."

The marvelous truth manifested in that incident is the fact that a so-called nonbeliever is not a nonbeliever at all, if there is love in her life. Unless, that is, we deny the Bible: "God is love, and every person who lives in love, lives in God and God lives in them" (1 John 4:16). This young woman had allowed the God who is love to reach her and influence her life, manifesting Himself, as He so frequently does, through other persons. "Everyone who truly loves is God's child and already has some knowledge of Him" (1 John 4:7).

This student's story forcefully illustrates for me the creative power of love. It also shows that most of us first need to experience love, then accept it into our lives, and then endeavor to discover God's involvement in what has already happened to us. Thus, for the majority of us, the sequence is: (1) experience love; (2) believe in/accept love; (3) identify love.

I remember being at a workshop on youth, when a

young man courageously stood up and said to all of us: "Will you people stop telling me that God loves me, and somebody please actually love me. Then I may be able to believe there is such a thing, and eventually, perhaps, I will recognize that God is connected with it all."

Even though disco is on its way out, *Saturday Night Fever* will retain its force as a classic youth film. Tony Manero's experience is not all that unlike that of my young friend. He, too, is pursued by the unrelenting power of love. For Tony, God fulfills His promise to be a light in darkness through the gentle presence of a young woman. When Tony makes his exodus to the outside world (Manhattan), Stephanie offers him friendship. This is something new for Tony, for whom women previously had been dance partners or sex partners.

Friendship presents another threat. "You've never been friends with a girl," Stephanie says. "Are you sure you can handle it?" "I'm not sure," Tony confesses, "but I'd like to try."

Tony was seared with pain and death. He risks vulnerability through a new life in an alien land. He repudiates exploitation and retaliation ("dumping," he calls it), and gambles on the power of friendship. In the last powerful scene, Stephanie opens her door (and her life) to him, offers friendship, reaches out to his woundedness with a kiss. And, in the final freeze-frame, Tony begins to allow love to find him.

10

The Threat of Love

I have been visiting a former student of mine at the famous Menninger clinic, where she is waging a brave battle with the demons of psychotic depression. It has been a heart-rending experience. Such a beautiful human being; a young woman I love like a daughter; so talented, with so much to offer the world. Yet she has monumental doubts about her value as a person, a self-loathing that, at times past, has pushed her over the brink into attempts at suicide.

The last time I visited her I was impressed by the change in her condition and the positive signs of growth. As she explained, this has been a very difficult and painful period of her life, but she has been realizing a great deal about herself that she never appreciated before.

As she herself put it, "How much the support I have gotten from my friends has touched me! I am even learning to accept it, slowly but surely. This is something that does not, and has never, come easily for me. I have never had much difficulty supporting and loving others, but allowing others to do the same for me was quite a different story. I am seeing now that I was really cheating people out of something they chose to do. I still have a lot of difficulty with it, but I am working on it."

I have been haunted by her words ever since our visit. Why is it we have such difficulty accepting love? Well, for one thing, there is something very self-satisfying about doing something for someone else. We are inclined to be more comfortable saying, "You're welcome" than "Thank you." We would rather acknowledge gratitude than have to admit, through humble thanks, how much we needed the love given us.

In support of this, we may rely on the old saying, "It is more blessed to give than to receive." But, in so doing, we may forget that it works both ways. If it is more blessed to give than receive, then we should frequently allow others to do the more blessed thing to us.

If we really knew the truth about ourselves, we would rejoice that others endow us with their concern and love, and would gladly recognize our many debts to them—for life, love, support, healing, and sustenance.

There is, however, a more subtle reason why it is hard for many of us to accept gifts of love. Again, it may be a truth problem, but this time not that we think too much of ourselves, but too little. We may simply not believe we are worthy of being so favored. Like my friend at Menninger's, despite many attempts at healing touches, some people still are going to go on feeling like lepers.

It is possible for us to be threatened by experiences that call for thanks. They can simply intensify our feelings of unworthiness. When someone holds herself in such low esteem, even a momentary tenderness can cause infuriation and pain. It makes her feel guilty. She believes she does not deserve to be loved or treasured. Consequently, when it happens, it's like salt in an open wound and there is a tendency to lash out at the person inflicting the hurt.

We may remember the girl in *I Never Promised You a Rose Garden;* or the dramatic scene in *Who's Afraid of Virginia Woolf?* when Martha attacks her husband. She explains that she strikes out at him because "he can make

42

me happy and I do not wish to be happy. And, yes, I do wish to be happy . . . and he has made the hideous, the hurting, the insulting mistake of loving me and must be punished for it."

There is a final reason why accepting love can be such a problem. It can be just downright frightening. To be loved means becoming vulnerable, allowing someone else into your life, and that's always risky. Even those dedicated to the helping professions (priests, doctors, counselors, teachers, social workers) have difficulties here.

I have known many priests, for example, who are quite comfortable as dispensers of services. They very conscientiously offer many acts of care and concern to others. But they never permit any reciprocity. They fend off people who attempt to respond with love of their own. They rule out all efforts of anyone else to enter deep within.

There is a great danger in this one-way-street approach. Those who are content to love but not be loved in return may find their love terminating at an abstraction instead of concrete individuals. For there is no way one can follow Jesus' way of loving without seeking to evoke a response of love from each person loved in the name of Christ. This demands a willingness to accept love as well as to give it.

Many of us are afraid of being loved because it demands risk and entails danger. A thousand seminary walls have echoed with the words, "Whatever you do, men, don't let yourselves get emotionally involved!" And yet the refusal to become emotionally involved with one's people, the way Jesus was, absolutely guarantees an ineffective ministry.

The challenge is profound—in whatever way each of us is called to follow the life-style of Jesus. He sought to establish a deeply personal relationship with each person He met. He literally proposed a relationship of love. But

He was always fully mature in the way He accepted love in return. He did not elicit a self-serving or erotic response, and always channeled the response to His Father, whose loving presence He had come to manifest.

Not an easy act to follow. But certainly worth a try.

11

Seeing Is Not Believing

"The church seems bent on making a horrible mistake. It appears poised to take a giant leap backwards towards a position of promoting a static concept of faith that will be catastrophic to the Christian community."

These words, shared with me by a bishop recently, carried a punch, not just because they came from a church leader but because this particular bishop, unlike many of his colleagues, is well schooled in the theories of religious education and evangelization.

He was referring to the fact that the church's current catechetical direction is contrary to the recent renewal of the church, which had been recapturing the correct understanding of faith.

In an earlier time, if we were asked the question, "What is revelation?" many of us would have been inclined to say that revelation is all the truths God has revealed—the teachings, dogmas, and doctrines of the church. Faith then, we thought, is the acceptance of these truths.

Unfortunately, this is exactly what revelation is *not,* precisely what faith is *not.* Revelation has always been, not a collection of data or information and truths about God, but the experience of God meeting men and women, an exchange between persons. Consequently, faith is not an acceptance of facts or information, but a response to this Person. It is the total and complete giving of oneself not to some *thing* but to *Someone.*

The failure clearly to understand this has led to great pastoral tragedy in the history of the Catholic church. It meant, as Cardinal Newman pointed out, that you had a lot of people who knew the content of their faith (the catechism answers) but whose lives were unchanged. I would call it the "Walter Cronkite problem."

A lot of people are willing to use the language of faith about Walter Cronkite. They will say: "I believe in Walter Cronkite. I believe he is fairly objective in his news reporting, and that what he tells me is true. I believe in the guy."

The problem is this: It's possible that these same people will go no further with Jesus Christ than they have with Walter Cronkite. It's possible to accept what Jesus says as true, to give Him intellectual assent. But this is a far cry from biblical faith, which is not a question of cerebral acceptance of truths but a total surrender to a person.

A famous writer of a few years ago, Gerald Vann, once shocked his contemporaries with the kind of shock we need again today, when he said: "I don't believe in the dogmas, doctrines, and teachings of the Catholic church. No, I believe *through* them in the living reality beyond—in the person of Jesus."

God Himself, as Thomas Aquinas insisted, is *the* reality for the believer. The current trend towards a static concept of faith, with its overemphasis on the memorization of the "deposit of truths," fails to appreciate what authentic faith is all about.

There is a content of revealed truth, which is protected and transmitted through the church. And this cognitive element, this knowledge content of faith, is very important. But it is completely secondary and supplementary to

46

the experiential, to the actual experience of encountering the Lord, who calls us to covenant and discipleship.

The current crisis of faith comes from stressing the cognitive without adequately respecting the experiential. We are in danger of perverting revelation, once again, into a thing, a collection of information, a mere body of facts. Churchmen once more seem to be on the brink of forgetting that revelation is an event wherein God Himself personally communicates to us through various means (e.g., Scripture, teaching church, sacraments, historical events, and especially other people) to establish and deepen a relationship of faithful love.

It is in the personal experience which is revelation that Christ encounters us, speaks to us, shows us who we are, and proposes that we follow Him. The fact that the current trend concentrates on information *about* God rather than on promoting in every way occasions to actually encounter God is the reason why informed persons like the bishop I referred to are becoming so alarmed.

"A static concept of faith," the bishop told me, "has always led to tragedy. Confusing faith with mere doctrinal knowledge made it possible, for example, for Catholics in Nazi Germany to have the best catechisms in the world and to be the most effectively instructed Catholics all the time that Hitler was destroying the Jewish people."

This same differentiation between theological literacy and authentic faith, between intellectual information and spiritual formation, means that it could be possible for a student to have a straight 4.0 in theology courses and be, in fact, an atheist. It is one thing to know facts; it is quite another to live a totally different kind of life because of a transforming encounter with the living God.

People who should know better somehow don't seem to

appreciate this. They might be helped if they took a look at how the whole business began. In the early days of Christianity, people would notice a Christian community ("See how they love one another") and be intrigued by what they saw. They would then go and actually experience the life. They would be touched and influenced by the presence of the risen Lord operative in and through His Christian people, and they would also hear about Him, all that He had said and done. Thus the two, the experiential and the cognitive, went together hand and glove.

Seeing is not believing. Seeing is knowing. We can find this illustrated in the famous encounter between doubting Thomas and the risen Jesus. When Thomas saw Jesus, he wasn't led immediately to faith but to knowledge, which is quite another thing. Thomas received verification that this was the same Jesus he had known before. The faith that followed ("My Lord and my God") came because Thomas was willing to go beyond what he saw. Faith is not even necessary when we see, and that is why there will be no need for it in heaven "where we will see Him face to face."

An amazing thing happens, when we take that leap beyond what we see, and believe in the Lord. Our surrender to Jesus becomes the basis for a new experience of vision. Seeing is not believing, but believing is seeing. Once we believe, once our gift of self to the Lord takes place, this belief leads to seeing, a new kind of sight, a revolutionary vision.

We see in a different way. The presence of Jesus within us leads us to see the world as God's gift to be cherished and continually created. We see in a greater way the importance of love and the significance of a life of service.

48

We see that violence leads to death, that peace is never achieved, only received as God's gift. We see that everyone else is a brother or sister. Believing, we see. It's a new world!

12

Let Go of the Bush

This past semester a friend has been serving as a discussion leader for a freshman theology colloquium. He tells me that his students are "issued-out." They don't want to debate issues. They want to know for sure. They want no more ambiguity and uncertainty. Anything less than full clarity is too frustrating.

His comments remind me of the challenge of faith and a story that has been making the rounds. A mountain climber was high on a mountain and he fell. Fortunately, he grabbed a bush growing out of the mountainside and hung there with his feet dangling in space, hundreds of feet above ground. He called out to his friend for help but the friend couldn't get to him.

He then called out to anyone above for help: "Is there anyone up there?" A voice from above answered, "I am here." "Who are you?" said the climber. "I am God," came the answer. The man was overjoyed and asked for help. God said, "I will help you, but first you will have to do what I tell you." "Anything, anything at all," replied the climber. Then God said, "Let go of the bush." There was a long silence from the climber, then he looked up and yelled, "Is there anyone *else* up there?"

That story says a lot about faith. We find faith tough. By it God seems frequently to demand the impossible. He keeps saying, "Let go of the bush." As we've already seen, it couldn't be faith at all without some experience of the God to whom we give ourselves. Still, we don't have the experience of sight. We can appreciate the words of the knight in Bergman's *Seventh Seal:* "Faith is a torment, did you know that? It is like loving someone who is out there in the darkness but never appears, no matter how loudly you call."

This was the experience of the Israelites: "How long, O Lord? I cry for help but You do no listen, You do not intervene." This is also the cry of the starving people of Cambodia, the parents of the child born severely handicapped, the student crushed in heart over rejection by a friend, or overwhelmed with loneliness. And it is the cry of Jesus Himself.

He had had an experience of the Father, and so had surrendered and delivered Himself in the most complete fashion. But on the cross He not only could not see the Father; He couldn't even sense His presence. It *was* like loving someone who is out there in the darkness but never appears, no matter how loudly you call—"My God, why have You forsaken me?" Still, Jesus was willing to "let go of the bush." He let go of His spirit in trust: "Into Your hands I commend my spirit."

It would be bad enough, albeit a lot easier, if it were just a matter of being hung up with that bush once, if we just had to let go in trust one time. But we know better. Faith demands we let go frequently; it means abandoning our blueprint; it means (just what that discussion group wanted to avoid) living in the midst of ambiguity and doubt.

If we possessed certainty, there would be no need for faith. Faith is a wild risk, and sad are those who try to destroy it, eliminating its necessity through their unhealthy quest for signs and miracles, visions, and apparitions.

The faith experience, that constant call to let go, will involve our willingness to leave the known and the familiar for what is sometimes threatening and insecure. The doubts that will come along will cost us, but the transformation is worth the pain. Reflecting on the growth occasioned by doubt in his own life, Dostoevski once exclaimed, "My hosannas were forged in the crucible of doubt."

My many years with students have made me extremely conscious of how real these struggles are in a college setting. Students, for example, wonder whether the long lines they find themselves in outside job placement offices on campus will simply be replaced by those outside employment offices back home once they graduate. They wonder if perhaps the only job they'll have for some time will be the job of finding a job.

During Vietnam, there was uncertainty, but not about what most of the males would be doing after graduation. Now more than ever, however, students are deciding their futures on the basis of the job market, a very distressing thing to observe. The phenomenon simply intensifies the already inordinate stress on grades, the often bloody competition, the sometimes widespread cheating.

The believer is called to go forward into the unknown. To do this as a student, or graduating senior, is not pleasant or easy. It means a kind of plunge, a scary proposition, especially if one is going to struggle to remain true to using one's talents to the full.

In times of uncertainty, it is tempting to be even more pragmatic than usual. It takes a special kind of courage to go forward on principles that are not dominated mostly by salary considerations, fringe benefits, material allurement, and a list of guarantees that rules out uncertainties.

One of the true joys of working with college students today comes from contact with those who, despite all the opposing pressures (especially from peers and parents), welcome the unknown and search for new directions, in tune with God's personal call. Those, for example, who consider new life-styles that might just mean less income, those who dedicate themselves in service to the disadvantaged through some form of social work, those who channel their futures as lawyers or doctors according to the needs of the deprived and oppressed.

The temptation to settle for second best, to compromise in order to grab a slice of certainty and, presumably, escape the risk of the unknown, is a strong magnet for all of us. We are all susceptible to the allure of certainty, safety, freedom from the unknown. In the midst of the painful exodus adventure, the movement into the dark and unknown, we can't help but wonder if God is with us. It so often seems we have to take these risks all alone.

There is a story about a man who had a dream, and in it he saw himself walking with God along the beach. The expanse of sand was like a map of his whole life. On it he noticed footprints. Sometimes there were two sets of footprints—the Lord's and his. But at some times there was only one set of prints. This bothered him, so he asked the Lord: "You said that once I decided to follow You, You would walk with me all the way. But I have noticed that during the most troublesome times in my life, there was only one set of footprints. I do not understand why, in times when I needed You most, You were not there." "My son," the Lord replied, "I love you and would never leave You. During your times of trouble and suffering, when you could see only one set of footprints, it was because then I carried you."

Often we may not feel that, but it is true. We are called to be willing to believe it, to learn that there is contained here a great lesson of life. Letting go of safety and security-at-any-price will make us vulnerable. It will lead us into waters uncharted except by faith. It will call us to take part in an exodus, sharing the life-style of those others who ventured into the unknown. Like a man named Abraham, and another they called the Nazarene.

13

Faith as Flight

Not long ago there was a series on public television about "Religious America." The documentary analyzes various church groups and individuals. The spiritual experiences are mostly private moments when the individuals feel they are in personal contact with God. For many of them, these experiences are in the nature of direct zaps from heaven—emotional floods of the heart occurring on schedule every Sunday. Exactly how these encounters influence them later in the day or the following week does not seem to have much to do with what these people are looking for.

Many of those interviewed emphasized that the value of a spiritual experience is precisely that it "turns you away" from the world and mundane happenings. For example, a smartly dressed parishioner in Manhattan is seen walking from church, as her voice in a narration explains that Jesus helps her rise above the ugliness and misery of the city.

I would suggest that this woman is typical of those for whom faith is a very cozy, private affair. Not a head-trip but a heart-trip. It is the tendency to turn in on self, to feel that once you know Jesus, you are released from responsibility in the evil world, free to relish the enthusiasm resulting from the possession of the Lord's Spirit. A turn-on to this new-found relation with the Lord comes easy. One can rise above the cross-laden life in this world to some realm of enthusiastic belief and ecstacy.

It is the problem of Peter at the Transfiguration. Peter was dazzled by this manifestation of God's love for him. He wanted to freeze the moment, establish his "tent" at that point, in order to languish in the comforting, consoling and exciting realization that through Jesus' coming and revelation to him, he (Peter) had "arrived." "If this is discipleship, Lord," Peter said, "I'm all for it. Let's settle here and enjoy this forever."

Many of the early Christians had the same problem. They felt they were already living in heaven with Christ. Forgetfulness of the earth followed and soon led to forgetfulness of the real Jesus. They concentrated on what Jesus was already giving them (strong feelings of His love for them) and, unfortunately, they overlooked what demands he made of them: His insistence, for example, that they now had the freedom to love and to suffer in the service of human beings even as He did.

The problem remains with us today. The basic mistake is in thinking that ecstatic union with the Lord in faith ("coming over to Jesus" or being "born again") indicates that we now have to live as if we were no longer part of this world. Overwhelmed by experience of spiritual gifts and charisms, the temptation can be to remove oneself from the negative circumstances of human life here in history—the "ugliness and misery of the city."

St. Paul sharply corrects this misunderstanding in several of his letters. He says that spiritual gifts are worthless in themselves unless they help build up the community and are inspired by authentic love, in the likeness of Jesus, who lived for others and fulfilled the commandment of love. Peter had to come down from the mountain of his ecstacy, and so does every Christian.

Paul's reminder still holds: living as God-touched beings here in history does not mean transportation out of the world but immersion in this world, serving others in order to overcome evil.

Real faith has very little to do with feeling good, a tingling up and down the spine, running around trying to get others to feel as we do. It is not a question of being painfully preoccupied with self, asking in every conceivable way, "How am I doing?" It is not to say, as some do: "Our responsibility is to save our souls, to come over to Jesus; it's not to get all caught up in that social Gospel business."

Frequently, this leads to a failure to live according to an integral Gospel. One may have made a decision for Christ and be willing to go the "one way," but be reluctant to go the *whole* way. These foot draggers misunderstand "evangelization." They confuse it with proselytism, and think it has to do with recruiting more card-carrying members. For some reason, they never realized that Jesus evangelized by *being* "evangel" (good news), and He accomplished this in great measure by reaching out to human needs with acts of love.

There is such a thing as a retreat to the heart that is the mockery of all true religion. Such a retreat is a travesty of faith. It is faith as flight. The temptation faces all of us. We hear that faith has to do with spirit and soul. It is supposed to put us in touch with invisible forces. Well, from there it is a short step to where things get very visible. Tragically, pseudo-believers think they can find a refuge in faith against the realities of behavior, performance or practice.

I received a letter recently from the South African ambassador to the United States. I had written him at the suggestion of Congressman Robert Drinan of Massachusetts to protest the human rights violations suffered by a priest who had been silenced and banished by the South African government for his work with the poor of the country. The ambassador informed me that what had been done was to preserve law and order and never would have been necessary if the priest had limited himself, like a good Catholic cleric, to "evangelization."

The ambassador was shrewd enough to throw in quotes from Pope John Paul II, but he cleverly eliminated any reference to the strong statements of this same pope (echoing Paul VI) that insist that evangelization includes not only a personal response to the grace of the Lord but also implies a deepening awareness of the need for outreach to others.

I suggest that the ambassador's interpretation is all too typical. It is to see evangelization as something totally consistent with the status quo, affecting only the personal relationship between me and God. This is a fractionalized and truncated Christianity, the sort of thing one sees represented by those charlatan television preachers who, while maintaining an infectious smile, spew forth their weekly platitudes. Their output is a commercial mixture of *Reader's Digest* and 7-Up. Everything is so well orchestrated: the unctuous voice, banks of flowers in the background, young, vigorous, perfectly-groomed singers, the local telephone number superimposed on the bottom of the screen, soliciting "tax-deductible gifts of love," as Anita Bryant calls them.

It becomes painfully obvious that much that is advertised as "religion" has nothing to do with God, much that is "Christian" has no connection with Jesus Christ. The cross too easily becomes a piece of jewelry, a pendant that hangs around the neck and decorates the bosom. One wonders if there is any room in this for the hurt, the crippled and the wounded. It is all so neat, the guaranteed neatness of a plastic product designed for mass consumption. How easily this plastic slides down the throat; but, like plastic, it provides no nourishment, leads to no growth. It is the cross of Christ compromised in a competition with *The Gong Show,* most of it fully qualifying as an "opiate for the people."

It thus becomes crucial to remember that we don't "come over to Jesus" and just stop there. If we ever really dare to ask Him how we are doing, He will surely let us know. He will inform us that we cannot join ourselves to the God of the universe, the creator and redeemer of the world, and expect that to be a private matter. Real faith, He insists, necessarily propels the believer toward universal consciousness and care for others.

To have faith in Jesus is to share life with Jesus. Come over to Jesus by all means, but then be ready to hear Him say, "If you wish to come after Me, you must deny your very self, pick up your cross and follow in My steps." To deny your very self means to put aside preoccupation with self. It's not so much a question of taking up a cross as something new, but of dropping the old false notions, for instance, that faith is a me-and-Jesus-and-to-hell-with-anyone-else affair.

There is no way to dodge the implication. It follows from the fact that Jesus says that we must follow in His steps. This entails the recognition that, once we share life with Jesus, we have His Spirit, which leads us to say what He always said—not "How am *I* doing?" but "How are *they* doing?"

14

Prayer Never Wins the Game

She was a senior whom I had gotten to know only slightly the previous three years so when she made an appointment, I had no idea what she wished to speak about.

I was, I have to admit, startled when she got right to the point and said, "Teach me to pray." She went on to explain that she had tried to be concerned about prayer through the years, but wasn't really sure what it was all about, or how to go about it. Still, she felt that prayer was definitely one of the things she ought to give some serious attention to before graduating.

We talked for a good while and in time a few things began to surface as most critical to the understanding of prayer. First of all, I suggested she get prepared for the shock of discovering that prayer is probably just the opposite of what she may have thought. It is not asking; it is answering.

This first problem with prayer is increasingly accentuated for me the longer I am associated as a chaplain with university athletics. After a recent game, for example, numerous people were saying things like, "You should have prayed harder, Father" or "Well, your prayers didn't work today, did they?"

When my prayers do "work," as, say, in a thrilling come-from-behind victory, what am I supposed to think? That the prayers of the opposing fans didn't work? The

God I believe in doesn't cause fumbles or help with freethrows, and His Mother isn't specially assigned to assist fourth-quarter heroics of Catholic quarterbacks. God doesn't win games. Men and women do. God's desire is to win people.

The difficulty I'm illustrating centers around the so-called prayer of petition. Jesus seems to encourage our asking for things. He explicitly says, "Ask and it will be given you, search and you will find, knock and the door will be opened to you." Well, we've done this loads of times and it hasn't worked. What is this, a cruel game God plays with us? We have engaged in prayer time and time again, but, more often than not, we haven't received any answer to our asking, searching, knocking.

Perhaps we need to persist more, one more novena, one more candle lighted, one more rosary, a few more Masses! Jesus seems to agree—in the parable about the widow who doesn't give up appealing to the judge until he finally gives in. This seems a straightforward admonition to persevere in prayer. We are called to be persistent when we pray. We are reminded of Robert Louis Stevenson's remark: "The saints are the sinners who kept trying."

This seems to put the major emphasis on our efforts to get through to God. We may suppose we are expected to wear Him down with a dogged persistence (something like a salesman making his pitch to a tough-to-sell client). We sense there's something wrong in this, however. We don't feel at all attracted to a God for whom we have to fulfill predetermined demands before He will respond. That contradicts the God Jesus reveals.

The fact is this interpretation twists things completely. The idea is not our trying to get through to God, but His attempting to get through to us. We may be inclined to think that prayer is our "working on God," but it's just the opposite. It works on us, opens us to the pursuing God.

Prayer is *our* answer, not God's. He pursues us and constantly would afford us an experience of His loving presence; He speaks a word of invitation ("Come, be My people"; "Behold, I stand at the door and knock"; "Follow Me"), to which we reply when we authentically pray. Thus prayer is an act of faith. It is faith articulated, and must always be reducible to "I believe in You."

We see that we need to persist, not because God is hard to reach, but because we are. We need to persist in our efforts to listen, to open our hearts and reply to His call. The Father whom Jesus reveals is one who waits for us to become receptive to His loving, saving, graceful presence. Consequently, that is the way prayer is "answered." Prayer is already an answer (our surrender), but once we do, God responds, too. We've given Him a chance to, by making ourselves accessible. And what does He give us? Himself! Thus prayer is our answer, answered! This is what Jesus says explicitly at the end of that passage about "ask, search, knock." He says, "If you, with all your sins, know how to give your children good things, how much more will the heavenly Father give the *Holy Spirit* to those who ask Him" (Luke 11:13). Hence it is His own Spirit He gives when we answer God's invitation with our prayer. We receive the same thing in every authentic prayer—God Himself. What more could you ask?

15

Prayer: The Essence and the Danger

I was at the hospital with the parents and friends of one of my students, who was dying of spinal meningitis. His parents came up and asked me to pray with them. We joined arms. And I began to wonder what to say.

Permit me a bit of background by way of getting around to how I tried to answer their request. First of all, it seems worth emphasizing the fact that it is perfectly normal and acceptable to mention to God our needs and special wishes for others. Even though He is already aware of them, it is still the spontaneous and natural thing one does with a Father.

The asking part is quite appropriate (the sort of thing we see in so many of the psalms, for example), and it may prove very helpful as a lead-in to prayer. It is important to remember, however, that what I may call prayer for myself or for you isn't really prayer at all if it's a mere request, simply an asking.

That is not the essence of prayer. As we have already emphasized, no matter how it is actually expressed, every prayer must have the sentiment of "I believe in You." Grammatically, then, prayer may be in the form of a request ("Be merciful to me, a sinner"). In its essence, however, it is more accurately recognized as an answer, an opening, a surrender.

The point is clarified if we analyze the request of Jesus in the garden of Gethsemane. He very explicitly asked for a favor, that He might be spared suffering: "Father, let this cup pass Me by." But that was not the prayer. The prayer came when Jesus added, "But not My will but Yours be done." Here He puts into words His faithful surrender, at that moment a most appropriate articulation of "I believe in You."

The request to be spared death was not answered but the prayer was. His prayer was, first of all, His own answer to the word of the Father, as Jesus perceived it through faith. Something, we might speculate, like this: "Son, I do not want Your painful crucifixion. But I have determined that men should be free so I ask that You accept the unavoidable consequences of Your mission to reveal the kingdom."

By His willingness to let go in prayerful surrender, Jesus opened Himself totally to His Father, thus His answer was answered with love. We detect this same concept of prayer in a remark Malcolm Muggeridge made in his book about Mother Teresa of Calcutta: "Pray, and your heart will grow big enough to receive Him."

In the light of this, it's hard to think in terms of "praying for myself," in the sense of a method of getting an answer to requests. It is surely fitting to mention my needs to God, but, if I truly pray, I am offering *myself*, not just my requests. Specific needs frequently are not answered. Surrender *always* is. In that sense, prayer is infallible.

What I'm suggesting is the importance of distinguishing between requests and prayer. There's nothing wrong with asking, even requesting miracles, but none of this is prayer unless there is that element of surrender ("I believe in You"; "Not my will but Yours be done") that we have been speaking about.

So, although I would not have hesitated to ask for a healing miracle for that dying student, the prayer with his parents had a different kind of spirit: "Father, we believe You are a God of the living. We cannot understand what has happened. It is a mystery we cannot fathom. But we reaffirm our trust that You love Andy and desire everlasting joy for him. We believe this. Our expressing it has helped to open us to Your presence, so that You might be able to support us at this time of our great need."

What we have been saying about prayer discloses also its danger. If God gives His Spirit each time we really pray, it will change our lives. We can understand how C.S. Lewis could write: "We shrink from too naked a contact, because we are afraid of the divine demands upon us which it might make too audible." What we find is this: With an old notion of prayer, a lot of people were inclined to leave their problems with God, unload their wants and needs upon Him, and then go on living as if nothing had happened.

That notion of prayer can weaken or detract from our service in the world. It can reduce our will to solve our own problems, by tempting us to leave in God's hands what has actually been placed in our own. For example, we may be so out of touch with reality as to say to God, "Please feed the hungry people," without realizing that, if we would only listen, God is saying to us, "Don't expect Me to take on your own task. *You* feed the hungry people!"

Actually, the evidence of the unanswered requests of those with whom I live points to the fact that I haven't really prayed. You see, God intends that, to a great degree, we should answer each other's requests. Say, for instance, you ask for bread. If I have prayed, I will be led by the Spirit given me to touch your life, to feed your hunger. God has answered your need by leading me to a new awareness and loving action. My lack of response to you, on the other hand, is a sure sign that I haven't let Him into my life through prayer.

Have you ever thought of this? If the enemies of Jesus had been men of prayer, Jesus' request to be spared crucifixion would have been answered! The Father wanted His son to be loved; but leaving men free, He took the risk they would not permit His Spirit into their lives, which would have guided them to spare His son. Consequently, prayer turns us out in service, answering the needs of others.

What a marvel! Countless numbers ask for liberation, freedom from oppression and poverty, ask for bread, jobs, decent housing, justice, ask for someone who will care. If they've prayed, while they express these needs, they will be open to the gift of His Spirit. And that is wonderful. But if we, too, have prayed, that same Spirit will move us towards these needy brothers and sisters, and a praying people will reach out to one another. Isn't that the meaning of that other prayer we pray: "Come, Holy Spirit, fill the hearts of Your faithful; enkindle within them the fire of Your divine love. Send forth Your Spirit and You shall renew the face of the earth."

16

The Divine Connection

Thomas Merton, dead over ten years now, continues to serve as a significant figure for today's college student. Shortly after his own graduation, Merton entered the Abbey of Gethsemani in Kentucky, where he would spent twenty-seven years as a Trappist monk.

When he entered the monastery, he was afire with love for God, but scornful of the world, the "Egypt" (land of captivity) he gladly left behind. Merton even used to detest his trips into town, away from his beloved refuge. They invariably made him disgusted and eager to return home. It took many years for Thomas to realize that to love God meant to love the world, to embrace that very "Egypt," the dust of which he'd shaken from his feet.

To love God with all your heart and soul and mind and strength (the first commandment) means to humbly give yourself to the world. That's the important discovery Merton made. The totally fascinating thing about his life is that, as he advanced in contemplation and became more and more involved in solitude and personal prayer, he became simultaneously more and more concerned about love of neighbor.

It was a strange paradox: the more he was drawn out from the world and into the love of God, the more God Himself drew Merton back into involvement with the very world he had left behind. He was, for example, most forthright and prophetic in his writings against racism, the evils of the Vietnam war, world hunger, the arms race, and our dispoiling of the environment.

The key to Merton's greatness was in his seeing and making connections. Why, the question became, did Jesus connect the two commandments? Was it somehow absolutely necessary to love neighbor in order to fulfill the first commandment? Or was it merely a test of loving God? Was it simply pleasing God, doing what He tells us, being obedient to one of His laws? On the contrary, Thomas Merton discovered that love of neighbor had a much more profound significance. He began to understand this as he reflected on the authentic meaning of love.

If love is the thinking, willing and doing of good to another person, we have to ask ourselves the hard question: How in fact do we do this to God? He doesn't need anything from us; we can't give Him anything He needs, without which something would be missing from His existence. How then can we assist Him, help Him, really touch His life, as real love demands?

Quite frankly, we can't. And that seems to be what St. John realizes when he says, "If God has so loved us, we also ought to . . ." What would you think? Well, if God has loved us, then we ought to love Him back. That seems fairly obvious. But John doesn't say that. Instead he says, "If God has so loved us, we also ought to love *one another*" (1 John 4:11).

I used to believe that St. John didn't say the obvious (our loving God back) because it was impossible, once you understand that love is actually affecting another person's life. I thought John was settling for the next best thing. Even though we cannot love God in the strict sense, at least in loving our neighbor we can obey God's commandment and thus please Him.

At that point, however, I became haunted by that scene on the Damascus road where a man, having been knocked from his horse, hears a voice from heaven saying, "Saul, Saul, why do you persecute Me; I am Jesus whom you are persecuting." Now, this Saul had not been persecuting the Lord. At least he didn't think so. He was a God-fearing man, simply doing his perceived duty. He was, however, persecuting the newly-formed community of Christians. It seems the Lord was making a connection between Himself and the people Saul was persecuting. Amazingly, God was declaring there was an identity between them, so that whatever was done to these Christians was actually done to Him.

Notice the way God puts it. There is no indirectness. He doesn't say, "Saul, Saul, why are you persecuting these people? It hurts My feelings. They also are My children. I consider what you are doing almost as though you were doing it to Me." It's true that we are connected with one another as brothers and sisters, and what we do to each other is done to a child of God. Realization of this would change the world. But the truth is even more earth-shattering. Not only is it a brother or sister we are in contact with, it is God Himself.

Jesus refers to this same identity when He teaches: "Whatever you do to these, even the least of My brethren, you do it to Me." Again, note the complete and absolute directness. He doesn't say, "I will consider it *almost as though you did it to Me*." There is a oneness; it is God Himself we minister to or turn away from.

When Saul discovered this connection, it changed his life. He became a new person—Paul—afire with love for others, realizing that God's union with His people made the impossible possible. It *was* possible to love God. The fulfillment of the second commandment actually fulfills the first. Thus St. John wasn't just settling for the next best thing. He was saying what we would expect (if God loves you, love Him back), but saying it in the only way it can be verified.

You and I can declare, "I love You, God" until we are blue in the face, but never know we are not just playing with words, unless we demonstrate its truth through action. How can we do this without involving other people? That's the connection. That's the consistency demanded. Otherwise we are spiritual schizophrenics, split apart, trying to go to God at the same time we tear ourselves away from Him by turning away from any other person.

This is what Jesus was referring to when He said, "If you are coming to the altar with your gift and you realize there is something wrong between you and your neighbor, forget your gift and go first and be reconciled with your sister or brother." As Louis Evely used to say, "We can't swallow the host at the altar unless we are prepared to swallow a whole host of people, all those we are responsible for in love."

We don't absolutely need one another to believe in God or to hope in God, or even to be loved *by* God (that is, to surrender in faith to His loving us), yet we cannot love Him in return, cannot love God in the full sense of love, as truly influencing another's life, unless it be through our loving one another. What a marvel it is that God has so joined Himself with us that we can, in caring for each other, also authentically love Him.

In one sense, as Thomas Merton discovered, it is easy to find God. Through prayer and quiet solitude, we can come to the point of allowing ourselves to be found, touched, possessed, truly loved by God. But should we ever progress this far, we discover something else: we

70

cannot stop here in some kind of antiseptic, self-satisfying isolation. To reach God and to have His love within is to experience His own yearning to love women and men.

To go away from people to find God is to find that the God within is turning us back to people. It is the wondrous longing of God to give Himself to the world, to touch its suffering with His own love. That's what moved Him in the first place to send His Son to save us. This is the lesson Thomas Merton learned.

It is the lesson of Jesus, too. Who should know more about God's yearning to give Himself to the world? When Jesus gives us His second commandment, to love one another we must imagine Him to be speaking right from the heart—from the heart of God, telling us (from the heart) what God's love is all about.

17

I'm Not My Brother's Keeper

One grave danger of college is if education is seen (and designed) principally as a preparation for making a living instead of a preparation for life. It can function for gain, not for growth.

In many universities the humanities don't humanize, they neutralize. Students are asked the wrong question— "When you graduate, what are you going to do?" whereas the real question is: "When you graduate, what are you going to *be*?" The chief concern should be what kind of person you will become.

The temptation is to reward students who succeed in acquiring information that will enable them to fit into our present system, with all its faults and superficiality, its consumer frenzy, and materialistic self-serving.

On the contrary, what is all our learning for if it is not to render service to human beings, whether in the most private and intimate relations between friends, lovers and family, or in public and institutional relations by responding to the needs for justice and peace?

James Forest, of the Fellowship of Reconciliation, says it beautifully: "The university is to be a place for helping young people mature into vulnerability." To "mature into vulnerability" means that the university becomes a place where truth as well as reality is sought. It is the experience of causing the eyes to see and the ears to hear what is everywhere around us, the cries of the poor and the oppressed . . . and to see and to hear in such a way that we become vulnerable to them and their needs.

Otherwise, an epigram of Bob Dylan can become frighteningly real: "The only difference between schools and old-age homes is more people die in schools."

The trouble with many colleges is that they indulge the nesting instinct by building protected little communities inside their great walls. A truly educated person has no walls between herself and the suffering of the world. And that doesn't just mean the world way "out there."

Let's consider a few situations. You are at a party. Someone, obviously smashed, is about to drive a car full of friends home. Do you let him go without saying a word, without doing anything? There is a girl who lets it be known that she is having an abortion. Or it comes to your attention that a friend is on drugs. Or you become aware that a student on your floor is starting to isolate herself from human contacts.

We frequently find ourselves confronted with delicate and difficult situations like these. Have we an obligation to speak up? To intervene? There is a much neglected (because very burdensome) duty Christians have. It is to become vulnerable to the needs of these people, who are indeed oppressed.

The trouble is that in our culture we have inherited some very strong maxims: "Mind your own business"; "live and let live"; "whatever someone does, that's his problem, don't meddle." A lot of us have followed these maxims and others like them so completely that we have developed a deep instinct against any form of caring correction of peers, colleagues, associates.

And such maxims do have their place. Minding one's own business is frequently the right thing to do. Who wants to become a nosy busybody? The image of the stool pigeon, the fink, the tattletale hardly stands high in our American way of life.

And yet there is that drunk driver. There is that girl going off to the abortionist, the friend on drugs, the student cutting herself off from life.

Perhaps we are perplexed not so much by the plain call of duty as by the method by which we are to react to it. In the situations mentioned, it seems the least we can do, and ought to do, is to approach the persons in question directly, to show them our very serious concern about the harm they are doing, or can do, to themselves and/or to others.

I know a student who approached an acquaintance who had drifted into a situation that was beginning to harm him deeply. He said: "Tom, please believe me when I say that I'm doing this because I really care for you very much. I'm truly saddened by what I see happening to you. I'm not trying to chew you out or admonish you. I'm not angry or irritated or accusatory. How could I be? I do crazy things myself, and need friends to care enough to tell me. So I've come to try, the best I can, to say that I care for you, I want to help. Can't we talk about it?"

That's one of the most loving actions I've witnessed in my many years working with college students. That young man had truly matured into vulnerability. He opened himself to possible scorn, ridicule and rejection. He was willing to gamble and to chance the pain that might result. As a person who cared, he could not do otherwise.

Have you noticed how often we accept things unquestioningly? Take the famous scene between God and Cain. He is asked, "Where is your brother, Abel?" Cain sneeringly dismisses his relationship to his brother: "Am I my brother's keeper?" Without much thought, we figure perhaps that Cain's problem is not recognizing that, indeed, he is his brother's keeper. I was jolted from my own uncritical acceptance of this by a remark William Sloane Coffin once made: "Am I my brother's keeper? Hell, no. I'm my brother's brother!"

It takes a real brother or sister, not a keeper, to respond to the needs we see around us for loving correction and care. Under the rubric of minding your own business, or even of never ratting on a friend, you may not be guilty of killing your brother, as Cain did, but you may be held to account for allowing him to remain oppressed in his self-destructive behavior without so much as a ripple of protest from you.

The response I've been describing is not different from the general command to love. But it is a most difficult and delicate expression of it. And a very necessary one, if we would manifest that we have "matured into vulnerability."

18

The Discovery of Fire

What we've said so far about the various facets of love of neighbor doesn't say nearly enough. Once we commit ourselves not only to the person of Jesus but also to His mission, we are obligated to a social response (our faith must be expressed in loving actions for others). There is another step, however. The Christian mission is not only social. It is also political.

For many years this has been a dirty word, and many a preacher has been castigated for "bringing politics into the pulpit." Acquiescing to the pressures of disapproval and intimidation, has meant that many preachers brought little of anything into the pulpit. Such muzzling of the full Gospel is increasingly intolerable in our present time of crisis.

Recently, thirteen bishops of northeast Brazil attacked the problem: "The church must side with the outcast. She will not expect to be understood by the many who can't or won't listen, even when they are faced with facts; these complacent advocates of the status quo, who form a private corner in religion, telling the church she must not interfere in politics and social questions; the people who use religion as an ideological weapon to defend the groups and institutions that do not serve their fellow men and who oppose the designs of God."

No one has led the way towards this new understanding and expansiveness more than Pope Paul VI, who insisted on the indispensable total dimension of the church's mission. "We must shift," he declared, "from a policy of simply alleviating the results of oppression and suffering to a policy of also eliminating the causes of oppression and suffering." It would be hard to exaggerate the importance of this principle of going beyond mere alleviation of results to the elimination of causes. This is meant to have a profound impact on our future.

The social response alone is dangerous. Simple charity (alleviating results) can leave the unequal relationship between rich and poor unchanged. It provides temporary relief from suffering without attempting to alter the system that is responsible for that suffering. It is the old Catholic "band-aid" approach, illustrated in the following case. There is a dangerous intersection, say, where serious accidents take place. An expression of simple charity would be to set up a first-aid facility, with no real thought given to lobbying efforts to get a traffic light installed.

A missionary friend provided another graphic example. There was a native tribe living alongside a river. One day, a dead body floated downstream. The natives retrieved the body and respectfully provided proper burial. The next day another body floated by, and they reacted in the same manner. For the next two weeks, the occurrence was repeated daily. Finally, one of the women spoke up: "Instead of just sitting here day after day burying bodies, don't you think it would be wise to travel upstream to see if you can discover the cause of all these deaths?"

The alleviating/social response is superficial in those situations where a more political response is necessitated, radical charity rather than mere simple charity. We are obliged to look not only at the immediate act of "giving a cup of cold water in Jesus' name," but also at the structures that made the person thirsty in the first place.

Such a judgment must be made even about so eminent a charitable operation as that of Mother Teresa of Calcutta, recent winner of the Nobel Peace Prize. While we applaud magnificent works of charity such as hers, we must also engage in a sophisticated analysis of the root causes of poverty, oppression, and human suffering of all kinds. As Pope John Paul II put it, in his talk at Yankee Stadium, "Seek out the structural reasons which foster or cause the different forms of poverty in the world."

From every indication, the majority of American Christians have not yet accepted the principle of this more basic charity. It seems only realistic to say that the shift to a radical charity that deals with causes is not going to be easy for any of us. It asks that we see things whole, that we ask the hard questions that will jolt against the superficial piety that is typical of much of our action.

It demands that we recognize that a charitable movement that seeks to transform systems, and not just provide temporary relief, will ultimately jeopardize our own privileged position. We will be forced to acknowledge that from the beginning human liberation has been central to our Christian mission. "This is what the Incarnation means," James H. Cone writes. "God in Christ comes to the weak and the helpless, and becomes one with them, taking their condition of oppression as His own and thus transforming their slave-existence into a liberated existence."

The trouble is, this brings with it the distressing realization that, as David Graybeal reminds us, "we Christians of the affluent Western nations are now more like the prison guards of the world than like its prisoners. And because we, like guards, are implicated and caught in the system ourselves, we don't know how, or perhaps don't want, to lead the drive for liberation."

78

The Discovery of Fire

It can, for example, be very tempting for a school, even a minimally Christian or Catholic one, to isolate students from any consideration that there are victims in the world. For if one believes in victims, one is led to believe also in victimizers. If there are oppressed, it might just be because there are oppressors. The challenge for higher education is to afford students confrontation with the fact that evil acts just don't happen by accident but have quite frequently been initiated by the will of those who stand to profit from them.

"The recognition of direct, explicit and not accidental causes and connections of this kind," Jonathan Kozol writes, "portends enormous danger for the conscience of the children of rich people. It is of great importance for the children of the ruling class to think of fear, starvation, sickness in terms of social accident or technological mistake; to think of hunger, for example, or the lack of medical care, like a season with too little rainfall, or a river that did not come up as high as usual this year. It is not comfortable to understand that the reason rivers do not rise as high as usual some years is that they have been diverted to the fields and irrigation ditches of another person in the upper meadow. It is even more disturbing to be forced to understand that oftentimes that other person is no stranger, but our friend, our next-door neighbor or our father."

There is then an inevitable anguishing of conscience that one experiences as a member of an unjust society. Paulo Freire, well-known educator from Latin America, wrestled with the dilemma; and felt compelled to declare:

> As I sensitize my conscience, I realize that my brothers and sisters who don't eat, who don't laugh, who don't sing, who don't love, who live oppressed, crushed, and despised, who are less each day, are suffering all this

because of some reality that is causing it. And at that point I join in the action historically by genuinely loving, by having the courage to commit myself, which is no easy thing to do; or I end up with a sense of guilt because I am not doing what I know I should.

That guilty feeling rankles in me, and it demands rationalizations to gratify myself. A North American theologian has called these rationalizations "fake generosities," because to escape my guilt feelings I go in for philanthropy. I seek compensation by alms-giving; I send a check to build a church; I make contributions, land for a chapel or monastery for nuns, hoping in that way to buy my peace. But peace cannot be purchased. It is not for sale. Peace has to be lived. And I can't live my peace without commitment to people. And commitment to people cannot exist without their liberation, and their liberation cannot exist without the final transformation of the structures that are dehumanizing them. There is only one way for me to find peace: to work for it shoulder to shoulder with my brothers and sisters.

This common effort means that, in addition to the financial contributions we make and the immediate charity we offer to those around us, we are called to renew the face of the earth, to enter into the reform of those powers and systems that are responsible for the plight of the oppressed.

That's what a real Christian does. Being evangelized and committed to the Lord, he can do no other, for he has been given the spirit of love. And this spirit of love makes war against unlove. Jesus' spirit of love is a sword, cutting us from uninvolvement and unconcern, a sword that separates us from the false peace of immunity from service, disengagement from caring, the retreat to isolation, to emotional ghettoes, mountaintops of ecstacy and spiritual privatism.

No wonder St. John insists that we can be sure that we know God only by keeping His commandments, His commandments of love. If our lives are given over to radical love, we can be sure that the marvelous dream of Teilhard De Chardin advances towards realization: "Some day, after mastering the winds, the waves, the tides and gravity, we shall harness for God the energies of love. And then, for the second time in the history of the world, we will have discovered fire!"

19

If Only We Had Known Better

The Barbra Streisand, Robert Redford movie, *The Way We Were*, has become something of a cult film for college students the past few years. There is an important scene in the movie, the one in the projection room where Streisand confronts Redford, her husband, with the charge that he has been unfaithful to her.

She demands to know how he could have done such a thing, especially with the particular woman with whom he became involved. Redford says to her: "What's wrong between you and me has nothing whatsoever to do with that girl."

In a very real sense, each of us could paraphrase what Redford said: "What's wrong with me has very little, if anything, to do with moral behavior." Not that misbehavior isn't important. It is, especially if it is seen as a sign and a symptom of a much deeper issue. The temptation is to get hung up on the symptom and fail to penetrate to what is beneath. For Redford, adultery was the symptom of a much deeper problem between himself and his wife. Dealing primarily with symptoms without ever getting at root causes can promote the transition from one symptom to another, from adultery, say, to gambling to alcoholism to drugs, etc.

The basic issue for Redford was the relationship between himself and Streisand. Jesus makes a parallel

point when He says, *"If you love Me,* keep my commandments." I wonder if we take that literally enough. I
remember a student saying to me once: "I hear that all the
time—'If you love Me, keep My commandments'—but
most of the time the way it's said communicates the
impression that what is really intended is something like
this: 'Of course you love God, so why don't you shape up
and obey His commandments?'

"If people who say that to me would listen to my
reaction," the student continued, "I would try to explain
that all of that would probably be to the point if I loved
God; but I don't. As a matter of fact, I don't even know
Him. So why don't you begin with the foundation? Help
me know God, and if that ever happens, eventually I may
even get to love Him. Then it seems quite reasonable to
expect that, once that occurs, I will *want* to keep His
commandments, or do anything else that follows from
loving Him."

The more I ponder what he said, the more I appreciate
the necessity of understanding that the failure to keep
commandments, our sinning, is in direct proportion to our
inadequacies in love. For this reason, what we used to say
when we were kids is still true today, and will always be an
accurate analysis of our sinning: "I didn't know any
better." The character Robert Redford portrayed in that
movie sinned because he didn't know any better; that is,
he didn't know his wife well enough. If he had known her
better (using "know" as meaning that deep, personal
relationship of love), he quite likely would have loved her
too much to risk hurting their relationship through
infidelity.

Here we see the key to what sin is all about. Sin is
always a sign of an inadequacy. It is always a symptom
that points to an insufficiency of love. As the Old

Testament revealed in its simple wisdom, sin is the missing of the mark, the failure to measure up. It is always the absence of something: the failure to love when love is needed, the failure to respond when someone is in want, the failure to be true when fidelity had been my pledge, the failure to take a stand when decision is demanded, the failure to act, to care, to forgive, to understand, to be merciful, to be compassionate.

When we refer to Jesus taking away "the sins of the world," we mean He takes away our inadequacy, our insufficiency. Thus it's not so much a question of taking away, as of adding something, bringing something to us—namely, the saving presence of the Father.

I am thoroughly convinced that only at this point of understanding does the sacrament of penance make sense. I don't bring my toothache to the dentist, I bring my tooth. The pain of the toothache does me a favor: it is a signal indicating how much I need to seek out the dentist. By the same token, I don't bring my sin to the confessional, I bring myself, the sinner. The recognition of my sinfulness helps me realize how important it is for me to seek out the Lord, revealing and opening myself so that He, who alone can heal my inadequacy, can work His miracle of grace within me.

The new rite of penance is slowly, but very definitely, beginning to become what it is meant to be for students. Once we recognize the truth about ourselves, we have a sense of urgency to seek growth and fulfillment of our destiny as mature, loving persons. And once we discover the true identity of Jesus, who simply waits for the chance to free us from half-life, we are eager for the encounter.

As a confessor, I find that students are aided immeasurably when I offer a simple invitation to help them get started: "What do you see when you look into your life right now? Where are you at? Who are you, really? Share that picture you see with the Lord." This approach seems to free students from that grocery-list method of the past. They are now able to see that the key is truth-telling, the honest acknowledgement of a basic fact that is true for all of us, from the pope on down: "I am a sinner." "Sinner" is not a term of opprobrium. It is a name of eligibility, for we are the only ones He came for: "I have not come for those who feel they have no need for healing; I have come for sinners."

Since Jesus never forces His way, never violates our freedom, it becomes extremely important that we allow the specific mention of those signs of failures (sins) to do its job of making us truly accessible and fully available for the continuing conversion and spiritual transformation that only He can bring about.

The communal celebration of penance is becoming increasingly popular with students, and for good reason. The prayerful atmosphere, proclamation of Scripture, effective preaching, appropriate music and shared participation can truly help us celebrate God's mercy and compassionate forgiveness. Just being with one another sensitizes us to the fact that most of our sinfulness is social in nature. Since most of the time our failure to love is manifested in our turning away from one another, a communal celebration reflects the truth that our reconciliation is with God and with brothers and sisters. We stand together as sinners, drawn back from our fragmentation and divisiveness, made whole by the unifying power of the healing Lord.

The social implications of so much of our sinfulness suggest also the appropriateness of confessing to a priest, who thus stands as a representative of the Christian community. But there is another reason, and it provides an answer to the constant complaint: "Since I can ask God for forgiveness anytime I want, why should I confess my sins to a priest?"

Of course one can always talk to God and seek His forgiveness and healing. But what about God talking to us? The experience is meant to be a two-way street. It always has been. God constantly has desired to speak to us in the most tangible, concrete manner. That is why He sent the prophets and Jesus, the greatest of them. God's desire hasn't lessened. What a marvelous additional dimension to the reconciling experience when God speaks to us intimately and personally!

This sacrament, like all others, is meant to be prophetic, that is, God, using the voice of a weak, fallible human, reaches us in the most direct way possible. We confessors, so obviously sinful ourselves, don't always offer the Lord much to work with but He has been doing pretty well with inadequate material since the time of Jonah, Peter, and all the rest. Students should feel quite free, however, to choose a confessor who *for them* channels the healing presence of Jesus most effectively.

Having said all this, it's a shame that the present form of absolution, though an improvement over the old one, still falls far short of what is needed. As it currently stands, the words of absolution give little indication that Jesus is even present, let alone speaking. The sacraments are Christ-events. Why not allow Him to speak directly, as He does through the prophetic ministry of the celebrant at the words of institution in the Eucharist?

The confessor, through his words and entire manner, should assist the penitent to the culmination of the encounter, when Jesus Himself announces the good news of His healing embrace. The following is a sample of what such a prayer of absolution might be like: "Jesus, who has been here with us, and who has listened to you, now declares His forgiveness, reconciles you to Himself and to the entire church, and draws you to Himself in an even greater friendship and love. He does so through these words: 'I forgive you; you have My love; go now in peace and sin no more.' "

20

Being for Forgiving

See if this isn't true. Doesn't it seem we frequently read the Gospel stories as though they were comic strips? Take the episode when Jesus says to the paralyzed man let down by his friends through a hole in the roof, "My son, your sins are forgiven" (Mark 2:1-12). Some of the scribes overhear Jesus, and so they throw a challenge at our hero: "It's impossible for any man to forgive sins; only God can do that."

Then we wait for their comeuppance. We wait for Jesus (like Clark Kent rushing to a phonebooth for a quick change) to reveal Himself, to dazzle the villains with a display of power and might that will prove His divinity. He doesn't let us down. He shows that He is even better than Superman. He proves He is God! The villains, we see in our mind's eye, turn away thoroughly vanquished, mumbling, "Curses, foiled again."

It might just be we've read too many comics, and unthinkingly desire Jesus to resemble too closely those paper heroes. Here's a dilemma for you: Suppose Jesus, at least at the time of the Gospel incident, isn't interested in proving He is God. This is not to say He isn't God. Most assuredly He is. But it's not for us to determine when and how He shall reveal it. Our constant temptation is to make God conform to our expectations and desires, reaffirming the wisdom of Talleyrand's comment: "God made man in His image and likeness, and man has been getting even ever since!"

Just suppose Jesus is much more concerned at that moment to teach another lesson, that it is necessary for all persons to be forgiving. Surely, God forgives sins, but Jesus' problem is to get the rest of us, who are unforgiving so much of the time, to act similarly.

Employing a very insightful interpretation by Father George McCauley, let me suggest that it may have been Jesus' intention to teach those very unforgiving men that all persons (not just God) are called to be forgiving.

Imagine Jesus wants to demonstrate this point. How does He go about it? He doesn't want to deny that He is God. On the contrary, He wants to deny the premise of the villains, the insistence that one needs to be God in order to forgive.

Jesus might do it this way: He might say, "Look, I take issue with your very principle, your claim that it is impossible for a man to forgive sin. You call Me a man, well, I believe I can forgive sins and I believe we all should do this with one another. To convince you that what I say has the agreement of God, I will do a more difficult thing—cure a paralytic—to prove that the endorsement of God, who alone can give power to heal, is upon the admonition I have given you to forgive one another."

I'm suggesting that Jesus, in this situation, wasn't into a "superman" role; He wasn't trying to prove He was God. He was trying to reveal the importance of everyone's being a forgiver. However much we might quibble with this exegetical speculation, it is beyond doubt that one of Jesus' major intentions was to teach the importance of mutual forgiveness. Indeed this practice is an indispensable characteristic of anyone who would follow Him.

Again and again He set it as a criterion for discipleship: "Go first, before you bring your gift to the altar, and be reconciled to your brother or sister."

So Jesus had to attack the fallacy that only God could forgive sins. Jesus refuses to go along with the pretense that God's forgiving is shaky or closely guarded, hoarded or doled out sparingly.

It may surprise us that Jesus is more interested in getting all of us to be forgiving than proving that He is God, and, if it does, it is because we are confused about what is most crucial. Jesus knows how important it is for each of us to be like His heavenly Father. Jesus, in other words, knows His Scripture: "You burdened Me with your sins, and wearied Me with your crimes. It is I, I who wipe out, for My own sake, your offenses; your sins I remember no more" (Isaiah 43: 24-25). Jesus tried to make this attitude of His Father His own. It became His nature to forgive. That's what He was for—for-giving. And that is what He wants us to be for.

The problem of forgiving is manifestly our problem, our hesitation, our reluctance to let God empower us to be forgivers. True, only God forgives sins in the context of the sacrament, but He forgives sins in many other ways, too, and He intends that we do the same, that our days be filled with moments when reconciliation takes place, when, through taking back and embracing the one alienated, absolution graces our relationships. Consequently, forgiving is destined to be our nature also, that forgiveness which saves others from paralysis.

This point is illustrated in the tale Henri Nouwen tells of an old man who used to meditate early every morning under a large tree on the bank of the Ganges River in India. One morning, having finished his meditation, he opened his eyes and saw a scorpion floating helplessly in the strong current of the river. As the scorpion was pulled closer to the tree, it got caught in the long roots that branched out far into the river. The scorpion struggled to free itself but got more and more entangled in the complex network of the tree roots.

When the old man saw this, he immediately stretched himself onto the extended roots and reached out to rescue the drowning scorpion. But as soon as he touched it, the animal jerked and stung him wildly. Instinctively, the man withdrew his hand, but then, after having regained his balance, he once again stretched himself out along the roots to save the agonizing scorpion. But every time the old man came within reach, the scorpion stung him so badly with its poisonous tail that his hands became swollen and bloody and his face distorted with pain.

At that moment, a passerby saw the old man stretched out on the roots, struggling with the scorpion, and he shouted: "Hey, stupid old man! What's wrong with you? Only a fool risks his life for the sake of an ugly, useless creature. Don't you know that you may drown yourself to save that ungrateful animal?"

Slowly the old man turned his head, and looking calmly in the stranger's eyes, he said: "Friend, because it is the nature of the scorpion to sting, why should I give up my own nature to save?"

Because we share in the Spirit of Jesus, it is our own nature to save others from the paralysis that comes from isolation, self-hatred and guilt by our ministering human forgiveness.

There is a memorable line by William Blake: "In heaven the only art of living is forgetting and forgiving." Perhaps Blake locates this in heaven because the art is achieved by so few on earth. Nevertheless, can't we dare to believe in the power of that Spirit of the forgiving Jesus within us . . . and what might happen?

Who is to say it couldn't lead to a paraphrase of Blake: "On earth the art of living—is all of us forgiving"?

21

Beware of Giving Thanks

Thanksgiving is getting to be a tricky holiday for me to get through. It can be a splendid occasion, a wonderful celebration. But it's also a challenging time. We can pervert the feast and make it a travesty and the same is true any time we give thanks.

Allow me to set a scene. I am sitting down for the traditional Thanksgiving meal. I am asked to offer grace, and so I begin to mutter words of thanks for various blessings, thinking myself pretty pious, without the least thought of the self-condemnation I may be performing.

I may never examine what it truly means for me to give thanks. If I am a typical American, I may give thanks for riches, abundance, all the advantages of the well-to-do. And at the end of my prayer, I may condescendingly say (and haven't we heard this a hundred times?), "Let us also remember those less fortunate than ourselves."

What could be happening here? Well, for one thing, I might be suffering under the same delusion as did the people of Jesus' day. They thought things like wealth and good health were evidence of God's approval. They considered them blessings, in the sense that they wouldn't have them unless God wanted it so. And they thought that those people without these possessions (health, riches, the finer things of life) were being punished by God.

Remember the incident when people asked Jesus about

the blind man: "Who sinned? This man himself or his parents?" Jesus tried to teach them a lesson many of us have yet to learn: Suffering, illness, misfortune, poverty —none of these have anything whatsoever to do with a judgment by God. Far from being a sign of God's disfavor, persons in these circumstances are, according to Scripture, God's "precious," His "favorites."

The truth we find difficult to understand is the fact that God does not personally bring about all these situations. He does not "cause" a person to be poor, to be blind, nor does He decree the opposite, that the person be healthy, wealthy, loaded with talents.

This should help us see that there is a big difference between being *unblessed* and being *unlucky*. Tragedy and misfortune are no sign at all of God's judgment or a revelation of His "unblessing," His curse upon us for some sin or failure.

There has been much suffering in the world because people fail to see this. I know a young woman, for example, whose daughter has been diagnosed as having leukemia. This mother has been driving herself crazy, going back over her life, in an effort to discover what she did wrong for which God is now punishing her.

Thus it is very tricky to give thanks for our "blessings." What I give thanks for may be something I should do penance for. Note, for instance, the obscenity involved in the action of those American pioneers who gave thanks for land they had killed for, land they had robbed from the Indians. The "blessings" (riches and abundance) that I give thanks for may be signs that I have withheld from others their rightful share of God's creation.

We are all equally blessed, that is, equally loved by God. We are not, however, equally lucky, that is, the free circumstances of life have worked out differently for each of us. What does it mean, then, when I consider those "less fortunate" than myself? What, in other words, does it mean for me to consider the Cambodians or the dying people of Mother Teresa's Calcutta as "less fortunate?" Are these persons less fortunate because God planned it, because they have sinned, because they are less worthy?

Feeling sorry for the "less fortunate," I may piously include them in my prayers and say to God: "Lord, help the less fortunate." If I truly listened at this point, God would answer me by saying, "*You* help the unfortunate. For, you see, many of the so-called less fortunate didn't just get that way by accident of fate or because I decreed it. Much of the 'less fortune,' the suffering in the world, is caused by those who are rich and who fail to share freely with those who have need."

The poor of this country, for example, are trapped and cornered, victimized by the rich, dehumanized by a system that inherently prevents a real political democracy. They are victims of a gross inequality that is contrary to the teachings of Jesus and what should be tolerated by His true followers.

There is a chilling line in the Gospel: "Teacher, tell my brother to give me a share of our inheritance" (Luke 12:13). How many millions are saying precisely that about us today? Those who mine tin in Bolivia and copper in Chile. Those who harvest our coffee in Brazil, the families in America who pick our food in the fields. All of these people, and many more, are asking today, and sometimes demanding, to share in God's creation.

Correctly understood, to give thanks for abundance is to give thanks for resources to be shared. To give thanks for talents is to give thanks (if we could but see the truth) for challenge and responsibility. It's true, we are the Elect, the Chosen People. But *chosen* for service, *elected* to get busy sharing God's creation equally with all His people.

God doesn't want us to sit down to turkey dinner at Thanksgiving, or to any meal, and choke on it. But He does want us to see that it can't be "dinner as usual." There are brothers and sisters of ours who are equally blessed (loved) by God, who do not show signs of being "blessed" with health, food, justice, housing, clothing, jobs. They are God's message to us that the goods of His creation need to be equitably shared. They are God's invitation to us, to understand that we are called to give thanks for the opportunity of changing the world.

22

On Getting Bombed

> "Wouldn't it be great if our day-care
> centers had all the money they needed,
> and the Air Force had to give a bake sale
> to build a bomber! "
> —*Sign seen on a college campus*

Students may not find it easy to believe this. Many people
don't. The greatest crisis facing all of us today is not
energy, jobs, communism, environmental pollution, racism, or even inflation or world hunger or terrorism. All of
these are critical. But, by far, the most serious issue we
face is nuclear catastrophe.

Unfortunately, most Americans refuse to believe such a
horror is possible. Even though dozens of top scientists
and political experts predict a nuclear war is certain *in this
generation*, it seems too unreal for most of us. "Because
of its catastrophic scope," Sidney Lens writes, "the
nuclear menace is neither believable nor believed by the
general public. It has been absorbed, grain by grain, over
a period of thirty years."

There have been at least thirteen occasions since 1950
when we almost had nuclear wars. The last near-miss was
in 1973 during the Yom Kippur war, when Henry (Dr.
Strangelove) Kissinger proclaimed a worldwide nuclear
alert and the Soviets were poised to send planes to Egypt.

Even these dangers of the past are far outweighed

today, however, as we enter the *second* nuclear age. By 1985 forty nations will be able to make nuclear bombs, and a decade later, one hundred nations, not to mention terrorists and the Mafia. According to our arms control director, the U.S. today is "basically defenseless" against this type of proliferation.

Tens of thousands of nuclear bombs, which can destroy the world many times over, are stockpiled and ready for use. Since Hiroshima and Nagasaki, the danger of total nuclear war has steadily increased. The people of America, Russia, and the rest of the world have been lulled into a silent acceptance of the existence of nuclear weapons. Despite detente, despite nuclear test-ban treaties, despite the SALT talks, and despite President Carter's call for a reduction of arms, the fact is that not a single nuclear weapon has been eliminated by negotiated agreement.

"What price power?" asked a recent *Time* magazine cover story. Unfortunately, *Time* didn't even realize the cruel irony of that question. They handled it straight. They answered the question about the price of power in a totally literal fashion, estimating the price of being a military superpower strictly in terms of dollars, $157 billion in fiscal 1981.

But that's not the real price we pay for our continued madness. The real price we pay must be seen, as Pope John Paul II pointed out during his visit to the U.S., in terms of the tragedy of handing on to our children, for their inheritance, the machinery of death.

The actual price of this is our sanity. We have lost touch with reality. We can kill everybody in the world twelve times; so we want to increase that killing capacity to perhaps fifteen or sixteen times. The sheer insanity of the position advanced by the Pentagon, the Congress, the

98

multinationals, and the White House is revealed in a single proposition: The more weapons we build, the less secure we are and the more precarious our situation, therefore let us build even more weapons!

The U.S. alone has put $2 *trillion* into the military since World War II, in the name of "national security." And all we've done is verify the wisdom of a remark Norman Cousins made more than two years ago: "The easiest way for a nation to destroy itself is to make national security the highest value. People are never more insecure than when they become obsessed with their fears at the expense of their dreams, or when the ability to fight becomes more important than the things worth fighting for."

Thus the real price we've paid is not to be calculated in dollars and cents. The actual price, in this age of nuclear overkill, is that we have entered the theatre of the absurd and abdicated principles of authentic survival. The price we pay for our current madness is also to be seen in the fact that our armament obscenity has meant less money and fewer resources for the things we desperately need. "Every gun that is made," Dwight Eisenhower wrote years ago, "every rocket fired, every warship launched signifies, in the final sense, a theft from those who hunger and are not fed, from those who are cold and are not clothed."

Our defense spending exceeds the total annual income of one-quarter of the world's population. Every fourteen hours the U.S. defense department outspends the annual budget of the U.S. World Food Program. The cost of one Trident submarine equals the cost of a year's schooling for sixteen million children in developing countries.

Even the job market pays some of the price. Bureau of Labor statistics confirm that thousands more jobs would be created by spending the same money on needed mass transit, better schooling, health care, and development of new energy sources, not on military arms. And yet, as Colman McCarthy comments, "You are accused of being a big spender if you want to lay out government money for people, but you are fiscally responsible if you pump money into weapons. You are a screwy-headed liberal if you want money for projects to feed children or to clean the filthy air. If you want more nuclear aircraft carriers or missiles, you are everything a fine American cowboy should be: tough, hard-talking and not one to be shoved around by the effete feds in Washington."

This is the price we pay for our present insanity. Military spending priorities continue to rob people of dignity, and even of life itself, while continuing to fuel the fires of inflation and unemployment. Foreign policies based on fear and mistrust continue to foster ever-increasing arms stockpiles. Nuclear arms continue to threaten total destruction. Non-nuclear arms continue to be used to repress social change and to preserve patterns of injustice, while carrying the risk of escalation from limited war to total nuclear war.

"What price power?" indeed! Arnold Toynbee, who surveyed the rise and fall of 27 civilizations, said on his 75th birthday: "We are now moving into a chapter in human history in which our choice is going to be, not between a whole world and a shredded-up world, but between one world and no world."

In the face of all these factors, it was embarrassing to observe the politicians in their petty debate over SALT II. Arguing over an agreement that would not reduce world armaments by a single nuclear weapon is as ludicrous as debating the location of deck chairs on the Titanic. The survival at stake will be secured only when we citizens insist that actions be taken that go far beyond such meager proscriptions.

Earlier (on the very day I write this), I was with students at Berkeley in a demonstration against further nuclear weapons research and development. As we stood in the rain, silently encircling the campus, I realized that, though the nuclear war so many experts now predict as a certainty may not come in my lifetime, it could indeed end the lives of this present college-age generation. I also realized that we won't abolish nuclear weapons in my lifetime, either. But we better do it in the lifetime of today's students. For, you see, we won't have any more time after that.

23

Turned off by Church

When students tell me they're having problems with the institutional church, I find myself saying, "Welcome to the club."

The problem is not in having problems with the church but in having the wrong kind. For one thing, and most importantly, students need to realize that some of their problems are not with the church as a whole but with elements within the church that simply demonstrate the fact that we are a mixture of saints *and sinners*.

But let's start at the beginning. We have already alluded to the fact in these essays that the most fundamentally critical thing is our belonging to God. In this is salvation and everlasting life. To belong to God means to open to His loving presence in whatever way we encounter it (for most of us as it is channeled to us through other people). This is our introduction to the kingdom, which, at its most basic level, is the reign/presence/influence of God, who is love.

Thus we can say that it's more important to be a member of the kingdom (that is, belong to God) than to be a Christian and, secondly, we can say that it is, in turn, more important to be a Christian than to be a Catholic. Response to God's "kingdom" presence in our life may very well, in His providence, lead to the further development that is Christian discipleship, and this to an even more specific affiliation that is Catholic.

It will be different for each person. All are called to salvation, to open to the coming of the kingdom into their lives. Some, obviously, come to a further point of (Christian) discovery and respond to the God, who, through Jesus, beckons, "Come, follow Me." Finally, a smaller group we call Catholics, in professing faith in Jesus as Lord, also affirm commitment to Word and Sacrament and clear membership in a community of believers with "apostolic succession." This last element entails conviction that the pope and the other bishops of the church are in continuity with Peter and the Apostles, leaders of those earliest Christian communities.

At this point, a couple of things can be clarified. First of all, in answer to the question, "Why be a Christian or a Catholic?" we ought to affirm the fact that one can only be a Christian or a Catholic Christian because one has experienced God's presence and opened and responded to it in conscious surrender. One need not be a Christian or a Catholic to be saved. This should free us from that awful narrowness and exclusiveness that contaminated Catholicism for ages. Instead of killing ourselves trying to assert the numerous ways we are better than all others, we can rejoice in the things we have in common.

Why be a Catholic? Because, in God's mysterious plan, one's experiences of the Lord have lead to this point. A Catholic friend put it quite well: "I just wouldn't feel so alive anywhere else. I know that there is salvation outside the church. But the beautiful thing is, now that I know I am free to leave without the threat that it automatically guarantees the loss of my soul, my staying becomes a much richer thing. Now I can simply admit that something would die in me if I weren't where I am. It's not necessarily the same for everybody; but, for me, I believe it's home."

Another point that should be made is that the expression "institutional church" is tautological. You can't have church without institution, without some structure or organization, precisely because church is community, an "ecclesia," a gathering of the people of God. From the very moment of response to God's call, even in its initial stage, one is affiliated necessarily with others. When we surrender to Jesus, for example, we don't somehow give ourselves to Him without simultaneously joining ourselves to those others who are also united to Him.

The vast majority of students readily come to accept all of this. As they put it, "We can buy into the fact that the church is people, that we are all members joined together through common faith in the risen Lord. We have no problem with this," they say, "indeed we gladly embrace the truth that we *are* the church, and that we are not to see the church as 'out there,' or as somehow the private property of the pope and the hierarchy, disassociated from the rest of us."

"Our problem with the church," they continue, "is precisely at the point of authority, that is, with the way the institution is run, with the decision-making procedures of those 'in charge.' "

It is here in the conversation that I usually find myself repeating, "Welcome to the club." This is the moment also when I suggest that a reflection on the authority of Jesus might provide a solution to our dilemma.

When the people observed that Jesus taught and exercised His ministry "with authority," they contrasted Him to the scribes; that is, He was not just an expositor —"authoritative" like the Encyclopaedia Britannica. Jesus' authority did not come from academic or professional credentials. Jesus' authority was in contrast with external authority, the authority people claim for themselves based on accepted badges, an authority, for example, based on rank, a sign on a door, initials after a name, a special parking place, insignia on a collar or a collar itself (of Roman origin) or a position held, e.g., boss, coach, superior, professor, parent.

We all know from experience that the effort to *claim* authority just doesn't work. We recognize that real authority has something to do with an interior character, a special charism. And the saddest thing of all is to see those who least have this interior quality become most vehement in their claims for it. The more they claim it and insist upon it as their due, the more they demonstrate futility. They speak, not with true authority, but out of insecurity and fear of being disobeyed; out of a dictatorial mind-set. Such a voice lacks authority because it issues its commands only from a position of might, not from one of right.

How was Jesus different? The answer comes from considering the root of the word "authority." Christian authority has reference to the "author," God Himself. God is the author, the one authority. Although I continue to be amazed that so few Catholics seem to realize it, the pope is not the supreme authority of the Roman Catholic church—*God* is.

No one but God has the kind of authority of which the Gospels speak. Everyone else, from the pope to the least of us, has something quite different, the responsibility, according to our calling, of deferring to the one authority, God. Traditionally, we have called this "delegated authority." Consequently, the supreme church authority of which we have been speaking can never be claimed by any person except Jesus, who was totally one with the Father.

The "delegated authority" exercised by all others is authenticated as genuine only to the degree it is a clear manifestation of the one authority of God, the carrying out of His will, the furthering of His plan.

Thus, from the time of St. Peter, all who have been in "positions of authority," have had delegated to them the responsibility of deferring to the authority of God. This kind of responsibility is not a privilege but a burden. Jesus taught, acted, spoke and lived with authority precisely because of His relationship with His Father; He had charism, the Spirit of God.

We can now appreciate something the history of the papacy has been trying to teach us for years. Faithful conformity to God's authority does not come automatically with papal installation, as though by magic. All popes have had the responsibility but have not equally deferred to the Author and done His will, as we note from history, when those "in authority" condemned Galileo, accepted slavery, outlawed religious freedom, etc. It is, therefore, crucial to understand the difference between authentic Christian authority faithfully exercised and arbitrary power. The criteria for judgment are the teachings of the Gospel, church tradition and the assessment of the Christian faithful (clergy and laity) who are promised by Jesus the guidance of His Spirit, "who will lead you to the full range of truth" (John 14:26).

Strange as it may seem, this discussion brings us to the point of asserting that we don't need less authority in the Catholic church, we need more! We need more authority; that is to say, we desperately need more instances when those with responsibility will more faithfully defer to the one authority of God. To want more authority is to want the Lord. It is to call out, "Author!" It is to desire (what

106

students and all the rest of us want) the coming of the kingdom, God's presence more truly manifested by His people, more faithfully revealed, mediated, channeled as Jesus once did, and longs to do again, through us, His witnesses.

24

The Eucharist— Why are they Coming?

A title like this would have been impossible ten years ago. At that time, and for many years before, the question was just the opposite: Why *aren't* they coming?

Now we have a different phenomenon on many college campuses, increased attendance at Sunday liturgies. As a matter of fact, there is a considerable switch from the way things were when I was a student. In those (ancient history) days, one went to Mass when at home (unless you wanted your father to kill you) but oftentimes slacked off while at college, once free from parental pressure. Now, however, the drop-off in attendance occurs when students go home on vacations, back to those parish Masses, many of which students simply can't stand. (There is a message here for parish clergy, which, unfortunately, most of them don't seem to be getting.)

What is there about campus liturgies that attracts students? It would be nice if the motivations generally reflected a high degree of appreciation for the real meaning of the Eucharist, but that's wishful thinking, I'm afraid. From my experience, I suspect that students are all over the ball park on this. They come for all kinds of reasons, most often a mixture of reasons, some rather superficial, others more solid—all the way from those who still come "to satisfy my Sunday obligation" or who just like the atmosphere, the music, the fact that "it's a good place to meet girls," to those many students who authentically celebrate their faith and joyfully worship their God.

It will prove more profitable for us to explore what actually happens in the best of these Masses, for, more often than not, this is what is appealing to students and beneficial for them, whether or not they are always able consciously and clearly to articulate it. Allow me to describe a few features of one of these celebrations, as it takes place in a dormitory chapel at the university where I serve.

Several days prior to Sunday the planning group gathers, consisting of regular elected members, plus the director of music, the celebrant, and the readers assigned for the coming celebration. They gather in a setting conducive to serious reflection and begin with a brief moment of prayer. They then spend whatever time is necessary de-briefing the previous week's celebration. This is followed by the reading and discussion of the coming Sunday's Scripture texts, suggestions for music, and plans for particular features, based on seasonal considerations or special circumstances (e.g., Advent wreath, lighting, variations in the introductory rite, relocation of the greeting of peace, dance, mime, announcement of a special collection for the poor, etc.).

The Mass begins at 10:30 p.m., but students need to arrive several minutes earlier if they hope to find room. They are greeted at the door and made to feel at home, as they pick up song booklets and find a comfortable space on the carpeted floor. For the most part, students attend this liturgy because they sincerely want to. They truly enjoy and savor this important time spent with those with whom they live, study, and socialize. They are already a community. They come to celebrate their unity in the Lord and seek to deepen their bond with Him and with one another. Thus, whether they all realize it fully or not, they are the praying, praising church calling out to God, "We believe; help our unbelief."

This kind of celebration becomes totally enmeshed with their lives. The Word proclaimed to them in lesson and homily points to their present moment, making sense out of their trials and joys, "downers" and triumphs. The celebrant-homilist at this Eucharist is capable of enfleshing for them the risen Jesus, who speaks a word to them along the way that burns within with enlightenment and power, as it first did for those men on the way to Emmaus.

This liturgy clearly becomes what it is meant to be, proclamation and response—God announcing His good news, protesting His love, illustrating His compassion, unfolding the meaning of life, calling to covenant and discipleship. It is followed by the response of the students, in verbal affirmation, gesture, song, and culminating communion.

The Last Supper wasn't the last one at all. It was, from one point of view, the first of many suppers Jesus would share with His people down through the years. This sense is manifest at the celebration I've been describing. The Eucharist is a time to remember, as is clear from the very word used to describe the climax: "anamnesis." This is just the opposite of amnesia. The Mass does not forget. It insists on remembering, recollecting, recalling. And what we remember is the cross. We recognize the cross as a slaughter. It was a "gallows meal," that final meal Jesus shared with His friends, a deeply emotional occasion, when all superficiality was put aside, when only the most meaningful and honest things were said and done.

We recall that supper and the crucifixion that followed, but we also believe that in the folly of the cross was fulfillment. It led to resurrection. Out of that suffering came new life for Jesus—full life with the Father. We remember *all* of this, His passover to freedom. It is this we celebrate, conscious that He remains in our midst inviting us to ratify the bond of love the Father would make with us through our communion with His son. It is in this remembering that we re-membered. We who are not all together, who are split from one another, our best selves and our God, fragmented and torn apart, are healed, sustained, made whole, joined and united through this marvelous celebration.

All that occurs within this Eucharist is to assist the participants towards a "faith-full" involvement. Everything depends upon this. Despite what a tragically large number of Catholics still think, the sacraments do not work automatically. Our dispositions determine whether or not we allow the Lord to reach us, as the tragic life of Judas, who was so frequently in the "real presence" of Jesus, makes abundantly clear. "Though the power to nourish us is in the bread of the sacrament," Durrwell once wrote, "it is faith that eats, digests and assimilates it."

The students at the liturgy I have outlined are led to faithfully and lovingly participate. To the degree they have been open to all the possibilities, they have had an authentic religious experience; the Spirit of God has touched them and transformed them. And, in that sense, they have had a taste of that heavenly banquet; they have, though they may not fully realize it, experienced how things should be with us, how they are meant to be all the time.

That's why these students feel so joyful, why their

greeting of peace is spontaneous and cordial and why the effects permeate their days and subsequent actions. In none of what they have done has there been empty emotionalism, fancy dressing or phony buildup. The Eucharist that Jesus gave His friends with the command, "Do this in remembrance of Me," doesn't need any of that. The intention has not been to go *beyond* the reality but to penetrate *to* the reality, realizing one can't improve on that. Jesus, risen and glorious, is with us, calling us into covenant with the Father through union with Him.

25

Sex and the Single Student

" 'Mutual exchange through conversation' is still a principal definition for *intercourse*, according to the latest edition of standard dictionaries." With those words, I recently began a class on the topic of human relationships.

Conversation was a rather common meaning for "intercourse" several years ago, but few people think of it that way now. You realize how complete has been the loss of that meaning when you find yourself reacting with amusement to a statement like the following: "The sisters shall not have intercourse with any priest without permission from the Mother Superior" (from a convent rulebook that, needless to say, has been re-written in recent years).

In a way, it's too bad we've lost our appreciation for intercourse as conversation, because it could be a clue to understanding intercourse as sexual union. Language can be a key for young adults in their quest for appreciating what is truly involved in heterosexual relating.

Our gestures, for example, always accompany relationships. What is the body language saying? Is what it is saying really true? These are the questions. Gestures are meant to reveal what already is a fact, not to cause the reality. The kiss, for instance, a beautiful and powerfully symbolic gesture, is intended to communicate something that is already true. Kissing never creates friendship, it symbolizes and expresses it. Thus you can see how unfortunate it is that we Americans have so cheapened the kiss. It is in danger of losing its specialness, as it occurs more and more casually and thoughtlessly.

What about more neutral gestures, like hand-holding or the embrace? A great deal depends upon the circumstances. A young man and woman embracing might indicate that they are lovers or it could just as well be the occasion of the death of the woman's grandfather, in which case the young man, through the same gesture of an embrace, would be communicating a different message, speaking nonverbally of his compassion and sympathy.

Intercourse, as sexual union, is not nearly so ambiguous. In the Catholic tradition, for example, it is an action communicating a most specific message. It says, in effect, "I am yours; we are bound to one another without limitation or condition; I love you totally and forever; and through this physical union I speak my complete surrender." The church has consistently declared that this is the language of Christian marriage, and that's why there is a problem with premarital intercourse. There will be an inconsistency between gesture and reality. What one is "saying" is not actually true. The nonverbal communication of coitus is meant to follow upon the definitive affirmation, the public declaration, of the fact of the bond of marriage through the sacramental celebration of the wedding.

The above meaning of sexual union is an ideal, of course, and it's not always lived up to. The gesture of intercourse can be distorted and misused, as can the kiss and other "signs of affection." Obviously, there is much less inconsistency in intercourse between an engaged couple than between two veritable strangers simply using each other for gratification, with no basis of friendship. Though there is a gap between reality and gesture in both cases, the failure and culpability is much greater in the second instance.

The most perceptive of students recognize these principles. I find they strongly agree that sexual intercourse is intended to occur within the context of the full commitment we call marriage. These students acknowledge that premarital intercourse may very well be precommitment commitment; that is to say, it may in itself be a very beautiful and highly symbolic expression but one that does not find authenticity if the factor of marriage is not present. And people can be deeply hurt when, as Rollo May puts it, there is physical commitment without emotional-spiritual commitment.

The sexual expression of intercourse is a truly wonderful complement to a human relationship, if what it says is actually true. The whole business is tricky because we are tricky human beings, and we can so easily kid ourselves and others. The principle of living we find in the New Testament is that we always are to do the most loving thing, but at times the most loving thing might just *not* be "making love." The most loving thing is, oftentimes, the most painful thing, and, for most of us, this most frequently forces us to be consistent with the truth of the matter. And if two people are not totally united and completely given to one another in marriage, the gesture of intercourse speaks an untruth.

Consistency between gesture and reality isn't a challenge for the unmarried only. Because body language like coitus is so powerfully self-satisfying, it demands strong motivations of love. Ironically, what we call "making love" can be very unloving and almost totally an exercise

115

in self-gratification (e.g., mere vaginal masturbation), if the partners do not focus their loving attention and conscious tenderness on each other.

It just so happens that when self-gratification increases so does the possibility of becoming oblivious of the other person involved. For example, every young man I've spoken with on the subject over the years has admitted that it is a fact of life that it makes a great deal of difference who the woman is to whom you offer small, selfless, tender expressions of thoughtfulness, but things change significantly when you're referring to intercourse. It is so explosively self-satisfying, it is liable to make much less difference who is involved. Thus the crude "locker-room" comment: "Sure, she's ugly; so just put a bag over her head, you'll never know the difference once you get her into bed." This is why, as Ernest Becker perceptively points out, "a woman asks for assurance that the man wants 'me' and not 'only my body'; she is painfully conscious that her own distinctive inner personality can be dispensed with in the sexual act. If it is dispensed with, it doesn't count. The fact is that the man usually does want only the body, and the woman's total personality is reduced to a mere animal role."

We now move to a topic that is even more fundamental: the question of heterosexual relationships at their most basic friendship level. It is alarming that so few seem to realize the critical importance of interpersonal relationships for normal growth and personality development. It is all but indispensable for human maturation that young adults have the benefit of numerous heterosexual relationships that are prolonged, personal, and informal.

There is no option here. One does not decide to exclude these positive growth-producing, defensiveness-reducing, relationships with a diversity of persons of the opposite

116

sex without, by that very fact, deciding to short-change human growth. We simply cannot develop normally as mature adults by cutting off one-half of the human race. Without these numerous enriching experiences, one is inclined to stereotype the opposite sex, treat them more as objects to be avoided than as persons to relate to and cherish after the example of Christ.

The male in our society, for example, is so conditioned that he feels a tremendous pressure for potency in heterosexual performance. The young student is encouraged to "score" with girls, to "make" women. This, Eugene Bianchi points out, is "sexuality of conquest, the accumulation of trophies to deck out his ego."

Unfortunately, this male mystique, with its proclivity to violence, emphasizes individualist self-aggrandizement through domination of others, as a sick escape from relating to women as full equals. Such confusion is the instrument that breeds bondage. That's why it is so lamentable to have seen countless students go through four years of college without healthy, maturing relationships. The lack of contact simply perpetuates and intensifies the mythology.

One aches especially for the more shy, the quieter student, who could benefit profoundly from contacts and friendships with his peers, but who, more often than not, sits at home on a Friday or Saturday night, or gets buried in studies at the library, hoping to survive another lonely weekend.

There are many signs that document the fact that today's student suffers acutely from lack of adequate familiarity with contemporaries of the opposite sex. One notes and sympathizes with the problem while recognizing that the developmental challenge certainly isn't met through such means as dormitory gossip, meditation on

117

Playboy centerfolds, or the perusal of television sit-coms.

No young adult will know much about a person of the opposite sex, even if going steady, as long as he or she is deprived of prolonged and rather intimate (in the sense of real, honest) informal contact with many. A young man, for instance, needs to know that woman is much more than an erotic machine. But until he has the experience of sharing his daily life with a variety of young women, *Penthouse* and other "fonts of wisdom" are liable to lead him to believe that "if you know one type of woman you've mastered them all."

Perceptive students will realize the importance of the willingness to take the risk to meet new people, taking the initiative by introducing oneself (in a classroom or dining hall), becoming involved in various extracurricular activities where one can mix and establish authentic friendships with one's opposite numbers.

All of this can be scary to certain students. Indeed, it can be threatening to any of us. There is risk involved. We all fear becoming vulnerable through our approach in friendship to the "mysterious other." But, paradoxically, it is only through that type of gamble that one grows and becomes the richly-endowed person God has challenged us to be.

26

In a Style to Which
You Are Not Accustomed

Recently, while visiting with relatives in California, I was escorted down the "richest street in the world"—North Rodeo Drive, Beverly Hills—with its parade of superexclusive shops: Gucci, Giorgio, Saint Laurent, Bijan ("by appointment only"), Vidal Sassoon, Elizabeth Arden, Van Cleef & Arpels. I couldn't help but wonder for how many students this street would epitomize the meaning of success. For how many, I asked myself, does this world of Mercedes and minks represent the life-style for which they will strive? On the other hand, I pondered, how many will make a decision for a much simpler life-style, in accordance with their sense of solidarity with the poor of the world? It is, of course, a decision for life or death.

Perhaps you've heard the story of the man who is having trouble getting through the gate of heaven. It seems he is hard pressed to come up with evidence of a single good deed he did during his whole life. Finally he recalls with jubilation that he once gave to a collection for the poor. The angel at the gate leaves to seek consultation, then returns to say, "That is correct. We found the record of your contribution, but we decided to give you your nickel back and tell you to go to hell!"

There might be a legitimate objection to this story,

since even a cup of cold water is promised a reward. Still, this doesn't lessen the shattering impact of God's teaching about riches. Jesus is so vehement in His pronouncement against wealth that He claims it is morally impossible for a rich person to be saved. So impossible, that "a camel could more easily squeeze through the eye of a needle than a rich man get into the kingdom of God."

For years people have tried to escape the obvious meaning of Jesus' words. Hence we get beautiful rationalizations like: "In Hebrew the word for 'cable' is a variant of the word for 'camel', so perhaps Jesus really meant cable. And 'eye of a needle' might refer to a particularly narrow gate in Jerusalem. We see, consequently, that it would not be so hard for a cable to pass through a gate in a wall." Unfortunately, this exercise in wishful thinking fails to gain authentic scholarly support, so one is stuck with Jesus' tough pronouncement. As Chesterton put it, we can commission our most ingenious manufacturer to produce the world's largest needle and our explorers to search out the smallest camel, and still it will not very much help our effort to escape from the full import of Jesus' words about the impossibility of a rich person's achieving salvation. "How miserable for you who are rich, for you have had all your comforts" (Luke 6:24).

Jesus makes the remark about the camel and the eye of the needle following His conversation with the young man who asked what he had to do to secure eternal life. When it was ascertained that he had already been keeping the commandments, he realized that this was not enough. He asked Jesus, "What is still missing in my life?" Jesus then told him, "If you want to be perfect, go now and sell your property and give the money away to the poor; you will have riches in heaven. Then come and follow Me." We try to water this down, too. We argue that, in using the word "perfect," Jesus was calling the young man to a very special vocation. We've tried to ease the challenge of the word of God by suggesting that Jesus was calling for a special vow of poverty. But we find out that when Jesus said, "If you want to be perfect," it was precisely the same as saying, "If you want to be a Christian, if you want to be a disciple." Jesus called this man to follow Him, an invitation extended to each of us. As John McKenzie points out, "The man does not become a disciple, and the only invitation Jesus gives him is the call to renounce his wealth."

Living under the mythology of that time, which held that riches and wealth were signs of God's favor, the disciples were startled to hear Jesus say that not only are riches and wealth not a sign of the Father's pleasure but a serious obstacle to entering the kingdom.

The disciples said to Jesus, "If this is so, then who can possibly be saved?" Jesus looked them straight in the eye and replied, "Humanly speaking, it is impossible, but with God anything is possible." We have exercised a final rationalization on this declaration, proposing that Jesus meant that by a miracle it would be possible for a rich man to remain rich and still enter heaven. But Jesus isn't saying this at all. When He refers to the impossible becoming possible through God's help, He means that though it is extremely difficult for us to free ourselves from the wealth and riches to which we are attached we can, with God's strengthening Spirit, do what otherwise would be out of the question.

Jesus makes another significant point about riches in the parable of the rich man who decided to build bigger barns for himself to store all his wealth. When Jesus speaks about this man being "asked for his soul," He isn't speaking about sudden death, but the daily account demanded from a soul, based on the response to the need for love. In other words, Jesus is not simply warning against hoarding great possessions, as though it is all right to be rich just as long as you keep spending it. Jesus is condemning being rich in the first place, a far cry from what some would have His parable mean, namely, nothing more than a mild rendition of "don't get stuck with a lot of wealth at the end, for you can't take it with you."

God's comments on wealth and riches as an obstacle to salvation confront us with a very clear and hard and highly unpopular teaching. Anyone who has tried to preach this aspect of the Gospel in a university setting can tell you about the cold reception it frequently gets from college students, many of whom (let's face it) come from very well-to-do families and do not easily tolerate any deviations while they are away at college from the "good" life to which they are accustomed. A priest-friend of mine was nervy enough at a recent dorm liturgy to mention in his homily: "You've heard it said that there are no atheists in foxholes; it may also be true that there are no Christians in Cadillacs." The sizzling stares he got from several in the congregation could have melted rocks.

Why *does* Jesus say what He does? Is it because He is trying to promote poverty (when we've got a war against it!) for its own sake, or because He is trying to suggest distrust and contempt for the goods of this world and material possessions in general? None of these. There is no merit in a kind of passive indigence or ritual nonpossession. No, Jesus presents a very positive Gospel and says what He does about riches because it follows necessarily from the commandment of love. It has to be impossible for a rich person to enter heaven, for if one is to gain eternal life she must love her neighbor and when

122

you do that, you don't have riches left over—not the way things are in today's world, anyway.

Being without riches and wealth becomes an unavoidable consequence. The whole thrust is outward, directed toward the need of others. A person who does this inevitably finds that it just so happens that when you try to be a Christian, you don't end up with riches. The Gospel is a call to gratuitously share with others, in the name of Jesus, the material goods we have, sharing them especially with those who need them most.

Even should we see this, however, and want to do something, our response may not come out at a radical enough level. For example, I've only lately discovered the real difference between real giving and a mere distribution of surplus. A careful study of Jesus' story about the widow who put her last two coins into the treasury reveals that the offering that comes from superfluity, and does not actually deprive the giver of a part of himself, is of little account.

It makes you wonder how many times in your whole life you've actually given, in the sense that it has truly meant a sacrifice. I was reflecting on this the last time I returned from having contributed some clothing to the Thanksgiving drive. I realized to my horror that I had gone through my wardrobe with a selection process limited to two convenient categories. First of all, there was the obvious category of things I no longer used and really didn't want. Then there was the category that cost me a tiny bit—the clothes I might have worn on a future occasion but wouldn't actually miss all that much. But I never got around to a third category. I never gave anything that I sincerely wanted to keep. I came back from this exercise in "giving" only to realize that I hadn't truly given at all! I had merely dispensed with my surplus.

"To whom will all this piled-up wealth of yours go?" God asked the rich man who had hoarded his goods in barns. The man was lost, for in turning away from others in need, he had turned away from the God of salvation. "This is the way it works with the person who grows rich for himself instead of growing rich in the sight of God" (Luke 12:21). A sobering message for our times.

27

When the Wax Comes Off

I've always had a thing about words and familiar sayings, an abiding interest in discovering the primitive practice or ancient custom from which they derive.

Take the drinking toast: "Here's mud in your eye!" I've never been able to trace its origin with complete accuracy, although a student once told me he had heard it came from a wish shared by farmers (if the soil is moist and thus fertile, mud will squirt up in a farmer's eyes when he plows). I must say, I prefer my own speculation that the saying just might come from the New Testament scene, when Jesus cures the blind man by smearing mud in his eyes. Since that action leads to such a marvelous happening, why shouldn't a wish for good things for a friend take the form, "Here's a toast to you; I drink to your health—here's mud in your eye!"?

I have asked any number of Scripture scholars about that drinking toast and the possible connection with the miracle scene. Not one has been able to solve the riddle for me, though they have been intrigued by my theory. At any rate, I'd like to think it's true, and have to confess that, if wrong, I hope I don't find out about it just yet.

Word etymologies are also fascinating. My favorite is "sincere." It comes from two Latin words (*sine cera*) that mean "without wax." It all stems from the unethical practice in ancient times of using wax to cover up cracks and imperfections in statues. A reputable sculptor or shopkeeper would display art pieces "sine cera," without wax.

That graphic illustration really does seem to capture what we mean by "sincere." And when we honestly look, we can see instances in our own lives when we cover over reality with all kinds of wax, facade, phoniness.

It is a beautiful thing to encounter a human being who is truly sincere. We saw an impressive example of it during the final days of Hubert Humphrey. There was a profound transformation in the man, and not just because the cancer surgery and chemotherapy treatments reduced him to a mere shadow of his former self, a shocking appearance that prompted startled second looks from all who saw him.

No, the change was in the inner person. Senator Humphrey was the same "Happy Warrior," still espousing the politics of hope with that strong voice and dynamic style. But something had happened. He seemed like a man free at last. He knew he was dying. He knew he would not be running for office (any office) ever again. "He knows he is free of the demands and the constraints of those seeking higher office," James P. Gannon wrote, "free to speak his conscience more clearly, free of needing always to think of the wishes of those he counted on, who abandoned him in the clutch. And finally, he is free of the suspicion and jealousy that attach to any politician who's believed to be racing for the top."

"What I do from here on out," said Humphrey at that time, "can't be self-serving, in terms of ambition. I'm going to be a lot more independent. I'm not planning on running for reelection. I'm not going to be making choices because I think, 'Well, this will get me some votes from a particular category of people.'"

Gannon noted how Humphrey-watchers in the Senate were sensing the transformation: "When he was going after the holy grail, he was always suspect. He no longer has that burden. When Humphrey speaks now, it is as a man who has no other place to go. And when he speaks, very few people leave the floor, and others begin drifting in."

That's got to be an exhilarating feeling—not having to play all the games that seem so necessary in order to score success-points. I can't help thinking how great it would be if we could be free enough to be as sincere as Humphrey was at the end, sincere with ourselves and with one another. But why wait until it is so late in life, I keep asking myself, until you have cancer or you're on your last legs?

A candidate for Student Body President once approached me and said that the thing he dreaded most, should he be elected, was trying to communicate with administrators. "They're so seldom completely candid with you," he said. "Their words so rarely reveal what's really in their hearts. There's so little sincerity." Well, they're not the only ones, I thought. We can all profitably examine our consciences on that. It is hard for any of us to reveal ourselves without wax. We are protecting our position, our job, our status, our comfort, each of us playing our little role of covering up.

Thank God for the exceptions. Let me tell you about two of them. Jim died suddenly of a massive aneurysm during his senior year. He was a young man known for transcending self-interest, filled with concern and tenderness for others. There was no bull in his life, no wax to cover over reality. He rose above shallowness and superficiality. Jim never lost that capacity a child has for wonder (how fitting that the day he died he had gotten up

127

to watch the sunrise) and he exhibited a refreshing simplicity.

That's another interesting word—"simplicity." It, too, comes from two Latin words (*sine plica*) that mean "without folds." In the past, dishonest merchants would try to fool unsuspecting customers by so displaying their fabrics that imperfections would be hidden in the folds. Simplicity avoids that subterfuge. It means being "out front," as we might put it today. Well, that's the way Jim was. Sincere and simple, a richly human and sensitive young man.

Mary B. is a recent graduate who is working full time as the assistant director of the social action department of Catholic Charities in one of our large cities. On a recent trip back to the campus, Mary and I got off in our conversation to that strange, puzzling Gospel text where Jesus talks about the necessity of His followers' turning their backs on father and mother and the other occasion when He said He came to bring not peace but division.

Mary commented how authentically these points seem to be borne out when one tries to be sincere (without wax) with parents. "I realize that when you are candid and reveal your honest feelings," she said, "divisions can arise in your own family. I have, for example, chosen somewhat different values and life-style from my parents. My attitudes toward them are tinged with rejection of their life of comfort and Dad's participation in a powerful multinational corporation."

Mary talked about the emotionally-charged discussions she has with her family: "My parents say, 'Anita Bryant is doing the Christian thing. We don't want your little sister to be taught by a homosexual.' I counter: 'I think the issue is one of human rights. How can we legislate that certain people be discriminated against? Teachers doing the hiring can still determine competence.' My parents come back: 'We spend too much money on welfare.' And I answer: 'But according to the Campaign for Human Development, only 37 percent of poor Americans receive any assistance, and that assistance provides for a diet that is grossly lacking.' This kind of discussion goes back and forth, including every topic from foreign aid to do I ever consider getting married and raising a family or finding a job which is more practical and secure than working for the church."

She paused and became very thoughtful. "It's really paradoxical, isn't it? Jesus indicates that for real peace and unity to come about, division must exist. We are asked to grapple with the seeming contradiction, believing that if we are sincere and loving even in our differences, the experience is creative, providing openings for conversion, a change of heart, a deepening understanding of Christ's message."

I asked Mary if she could see any of this verified in her relationship with her own parents. "Yes, I believe so," she answered. "It's not a comfortable teaching, but Jesus tells us that we must be willing to turn away even from family if that's what it takes to sincerely respond to His call. Though we are tempted at times, due to frustration and hurt, to cop out of our struggle to be sincere with each other, my parents and I will continue to deal as honestly as we can with our differences.

"We are committed to that struggle," Mary concluded, "because we have seen its creativity, which has been reflected in deepening love and changes of attitude. But we also know that we have to be willing to let go of each other, and that the letting go will not mean that we have loved any less."

28

Exit Laughing

One of the most distressing things about our present moment is the high number of humorless, sad Christians peopling the land. These are the folks who are into the rigors of the law. They are heavy on moralism and legalism. They like to quote the rebuking and reprimanding passages of Scripture. They are joyless, smileless Old Testament Christians (and that, of course, is a contradiction in terms).

I wish they could learn something from Lazarus. You see, Lazarus came out of the tomb laughing. He had discovered the answer to the question, "What happens when you die?" Lazarus realized that death was not the end, but just the beginning of life everlasting. He would, for the rest of his life, share that discovery with people, building up their hope. And when he died (the final time), he died laughing, for he'd already faced death before and so didn't fear it any more.

The lesson that Lazarus would teach us is the lesson of hope—the hope that comes from trusting that God's grace is being poured out on the world, hope that what should be shall be, confident that the future is not entirely in human hands but in the hands of a certain Carpenter who wept at the grave of Lazarus and called him forth.

In the light of such hope, and with the assurance of a liberating God, one can laugh at the human folly in each and every one of us, even in the midst of misery. Life is meant to have that sort of balance, that type of tension. At one and the same time we can say what a fabulous world this is and what an unbelievably crummy world it is. We are called to deal with this dilemma, to recognize that life is not absurd but ambiguous, filled with many meanings, some of which appear contradictory.

Humor is the great leveler. It can help us laugh at ourselves and our foibles with the same patience and gentleness with which God must laugh at us. But such humor is easily misunderstood, even apt to scandalize moralistic and critical minds. No wonder Gilbert Chesterton shocked the world of his time when he suggested that Jesus withdrew into the desert because He could no longer control His laughter and knew that His mirth and joy would only be misunderstood.

Hope does marvelously strange things to us. Regrettably, a lot of people aren't ready for it. To them we will seem to be out of touch and unsympathetic to the misery and sinfulness in the world, or malicious in our laughter at the expense of misery, or just downright uncaring.

Herb Gardner, in his enchanting play *A Thousand Clowns*, has his main character, Murray, comment on his nephew. "He is a laugher, and laughers are rare. I mean, you tell that kid something funny . . . not just any piece of corn, but something funny, and he'll give you your money's worth. It's not just funny jokes he reads, or I tell him, that he laughs at. Not just setup funny stuff. He sees street jokes, he has the good eye, he sees subway farce and crosstown-bus humor and all the cartoons that people make by being alive. He has a good eye."

Lazarus had a good eye! He realized that he was not raised up in resurrection; something quite different had happened to him. He was resuscitated, reclaimed, returned to a still mortal world with its taxes and burdens and painful trials. And he would still have to die. So he was right back where he started . . . but not exactly. For Lazarus had seen enough on the other side to make him a man of hope. And he would pass it on: God *is* love; He *does* care; He frees His people. All the promises are true!

We ourselves are meant to come to a point where we refuse to believe that God, who has constantly been offering us more life, would be such a monster as to suddenly reverse the process at the end. He is the God of the living. Since our destiny of full life can't be reached until the final breakthrough, physical death is not the end, but the end of all those steps of breaking forth into new life through deaths—as a child, adolescent, adult.

As a matter of fact, that final step of physical death is really our last step in being born. Let me illustrate the point.

A short while back, a priest-friend of mine died of cancer. He was a truly wonderful man, a compassionate and loving servant of people. But he saved the best for last. During those final weeks of lingering suffering, he gave a tremendous example of courage, trust and hope to all of us who spent time with him. He began to slip fast and everybody knew it was just a matter of a few days. Then somebody recalled that his birthday was approaching and we all began to wonder if we were about to witness a strange coincidence.

It happened that way. Father Ed died on his birthday. And, once again, we were confronted with a powerful truth of Christian tradition. In the history of the church, saints most frequently are commemorated on the day they died, for that, in the belief of Christians, is truly the day they are born into heaven.

Through a startling coincidence, Father Ed's birthday

became his day of birth! In a true sense, all of life is meant to be seen as life in the womb. All our failures and frailties are like the floundering of the unborn child. In this life we still share some of the helplessness and dependency of the unborn. Only with the final breakthrough and passover at death do we become fully alive.

To have witnessed a death-into-life like that of Father Ed, is to become convinced of the reasonableness of our hope. It is to affirm that a God who regenerates the earth each spring will surely raise up His sons and daughters.

And so we finally come to see that at the end we are just beginning. It's not "dearly departed," but "newly arrived." It is to know forever that He wasn't kidding when He said, "I have come that you might have life, and have it to the full."